DON'T MISS THESE OTHER TRUE RESCUE STORIES

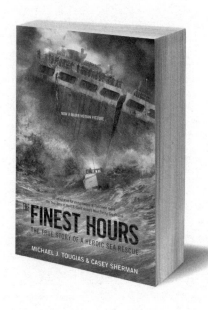

A *New York Times* Bestseller

An Amazon Best Book of the Month

A Junior Library Guild Selection

"A thrilling, harrowing account of disaster and heroism."
—*Kirkus Reviews*

"This poignant history should be an easy sell to readers of adventure, seafaring, or rescue stories."
—*School Library Journal*

"Nail-biting and . . . invigorating."
—*Booklist*

A Junior Library Guild Selection

A Scholastic Book Club Selection

A Cybil's Award Finalist

"A sure-fire hit with young readers who are always ready for a good disaster tale." —*Kirkus Reviews*

"The dramatic narrative is engaging and won't disappoint students who enjoy adventure or rescue stories."
—*School Library Journal*

"This true story . . . reads like a thriller, with one thing after another going wrong and each challenge seemingly impossible to overcome." —*Booklist*

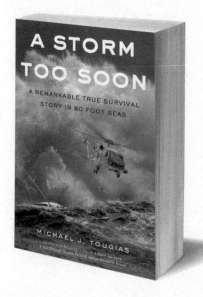

INTO THE
BLIZZARD

INTO THE BLIZZARD

HEROISM AT SEA DURING THE GREAT BLIZZARD OF 1978

An adaptation for young readers of the national bestseller
*Ten Hours Until Dawn: The True Story of Heroism and Tragedy
Aboard the* Can Do

MICHAEL J. TOUGIAS

Christy Ottaviano Books
Henry Holt and Company
New York

Henry Holt and Company, *Publishers since 1866*
Henry Holt® is a registered trademark of Macmillan Publishing Group, LLC
120 Broadway, New York, NY 10271 • mackids.com

ISBN 978-1-62779-283-7
Library of Congress Control Number 2019932420

Our books may be purchased in bulk for promotional, educational, or business use.
Please contact your local bookseller or the Macmillan Corporate and Premium Sales
Department at (800) 221-7945 ext. 5442 or by email at MacmillanSpecialMarkets@
macmillan.com.

First edition, 2019 / Designed by Liz Dresner
Printed in the United States of America by LSC Communications,
Harrisonburg, Virginia

10 9 8 7 6 5 4 3 2 1

To the men on board the Can Do: *Frank E. Quirk II, Charles Bucko,*
Kenneth Fuller Jr., Norman David Curley, and Donald Wilkinson.
And to Gard Estes and the men and women of the U.S. Coast Guard,
who put their lives on the line helping others.

I believe that man will not merely endure: he will prevail.
He is immortal, not because he alone among creatures
has an inexhaustible voice, but because he has a soul, a
spirit capable of compassion and sacrifice and endurance.

—WILLIAM FAULKNER

CONTENTS

PROLOGUE

Samuel de Champlain discovered Gloucester Harbor in 1606 and named it Le Beauport, the beautiful port. For weary sailors it is just that. A mile wide and almost two miles long, the harbor is sheltered by land on three sides and is one of the best ports on the northeast coast. From Champlain's discovery up to the year 1905, a long and dangerous shoal, Dog Bar Shoal, extended almost halfway across the harbor's opening to the ocean.

Although the harbor offered safety, some storms were so powerful their fury reached inside the harbor by sending tremendous seas through the opening and over the shoal. In 1839 a great gale slammed into the port, crashing at least twenty schooners along the western shore. Witnesses said that intermittently above the tumult they heard the cries of perishing sailors pleading for help. Some were drowned and dashed upon the harbor's surrounding ledges, while others were swept up and over Dog Bar Shoal and sent tumbling out to sea. In 1898 another gale breached the harbor, resulting in the loss of at least twenty lives within its confines. Author Joseph Garland, in *Down to the Sea*, likened the mariners' deaths to "drowning in the bathtub." Because of these events, at the turn of the century, construction of a breakwater began. Granite blocks and rocks were positioned atop the shoal. The finished seawall, called Dog Bar Breakwater, was completed in 1905, and it, along with the adjacent granite mass known as Eastern Point, made the harbor considerably safer, protecting it from the full fury of northeast winds.

In 1978 Gloucester Harbor was still a beautiful and active port. Tankers, freighters, fishing vessels, and pleasure boats were continuously entering or exiting its calm waters. Because of their great size, the tankers and freighters had to be guided through the harbor by local pilots who had intimate knowledge of its depths and hazards. The pilots were brought out to ships aboard a forty-nine-foot pilot boat called the *Can Do*, captained by Frank E. Quirk II. Frank would pull the *Can Do* alongside a huge ship, and the pilot then climbed a dangling rope ladder to board the vessel. Once the pilot was on board, he would take over the controls, maneuvering the vessel to port. Frank sometimes led the way in the *Can Do*, communicating with the pilot by radio to ensure a safe entry. Often the *Can Do* would be involved in the final docking, nudging the ship into the proper position.

Although the *Can Do*'s dock slip was in Gloucester's South Channel off Rogers Street near the Coast Guard station, Frank also serviced Salem Harbor, just fifteen miles to the south. It was there, on February 1, that Frank helped guide in a huge 685-foot Greek-registered oil tanker. The tanker was named the *Global*

Hope, and its cargo of oil was to be off-loaded at a power plant. The job was a routine one for Frank, and he thought the next time he'd hear from the tanker would be when it was ready to leave and a pilot was needed.

Instead, fate, the actions of the tanker's captain, and a blizzard of incredible fury set in motion events that spiraled out of control.

KEY VESSELS AND CREW MEMBERS

Can Do: A 49-foot pilot boat with Captain Frank E. Quirk II, Charles Bucko, Kenneth Fuller Jr., Norman David Curley, and Donald Wilkinson aboard.

Coast Guard 44-foot motor lifeboat: "The Forty-Four." A frequently used rescue boat carrying seamen Robert Krom and Roger Mathurin, engineer Tom Desrosiers, and skipper/coxswain Bob McIlvride.

Global Hope: a Greek-registered oil tanker, 682 feet in length, with a crew of 32 men.

Coast Guard cutter *Cape George*: 95 feet; key crew members include Dennis Hoffer, Glen Snyder, Myron Verville, Bob Donovan, and Vern DePietro. (The *Cape George* was the same type of cutter shown here.)

Coast Guard cutter *Decisive*: 210 feet; key crew members include Jim Quinn, Rich Fitcher, and Jim Sawyer. (The *Decisive* was the same type of cutter shown here.)

PART 1

THE GATHERING STORM

Frank Quirk often spent the night aboard the *Can Do*. On the morning of February 6, 1978, he awoke wondering when it would snow. The prior evening's weather forecast called for snowfall to begin in the early morning hours, yet there wasn't a flake in the sky, just low, leaden clouds and a bitter cold breeze. He could have caught a little more sleep, because no piloting jobs were scheduled, but that wasn't his nature. The forty-nine-year-old former Navy Seabee (Seabee, as in CB—construction battalion—a force that builds whatever the military needs, such as bridges or hospitals), with a wife and three children, was disciplined and full of energy. Although Frank's crew-cut hair was mostly gray, he kept in tip-top shape and was quite strong, with a stocky build. He was well liked, with an easygoing manner and a ready smile.

Frank had been plying these waters for over twenty years and had a healthy respect for the sea. He considered himself fortunate: his work allowed him to be his own boss, and instead of laboring in an office, he could be on the ocean nearly every day. Frank loved the sea, both the freedom it afforded as well as its challenges and ever-changing nature. He felt the same about the *Can Do*, which he had named with the Seabees' motto.

Among Gloucester's fishing and boating community, Frank was well known. He had received two Mariner's Medals for heroism at sea and countless times aided boaters in distress. Sometimes he just brought fuel to a skipper who had run out of gas, or dived overboard to retrieve a pair of eyeglasses dropped by a careless boater. One recreational boater recalled radioing for assistance when the engine on his motorboat conked out on a beautiful Saturday afternoon. Frank was relaxing on the *Can Do*, several miles away. When no boaters close to the motorboat came on the radio, Frank went on the air, offering a tow from Gloucester to the boat's home port in Marblehead, several miles away. The tow and return trip consumed six or seven hours of Frank's day off, but he refused to accept any payment. He usually just said, "It was nothing at all," or if the boat had fishermen aboard, "Just throw me a fish next time you see me." His kids said Frank brought home a lot of fish and lobsters.

On that Monday morning, Frank was listening to the marine

radio in the *Can Do*'s wheelhouse. Surrounded by small rectangular glass windows, he had a good view of Gloucester's inner harbor, where all manner of boats were docked, from battered and rusting fishing trawlers to sleek, modern pleasure yachts. The National Weather Service was announcing an updated forecast, saying the snow was still coming and would be accompanied by high winds. Meteorologists explained that the snowfall could be significant, and some even used the term *blizzard*, but few gave any inkling that New Englanders were about to be pounded by a blizzard of incredible proportions. New England's "storm of the century" was on the way, heading directly up the Eastern Seaboard toward Massachusetts.

The storm was a deceptive one at this early stage. It was located off the Maryland coast, and during the morning hours, the mid-Atlantic states as well as New Jersey and New York were receiving significant snowfall accompanied by strong winds. This region, however, was absorbing just a glancing blow compared to what was in store for Massachusetts and Rhode Island, because with each passing hour, the storm intensified. The storm was strengthening so rapidly, meteorologists later would refer to it as a "bombogenesis" or simply a bomb. As it moved north, winds would go from "strong" to hurricane force, clocked at a ferocious ninety-two miles per hour when they reached Massachusetts. Winds of this magnitude caught everyone off guard. And no meteorologist predicted the other surprise the storm had in store—that it would stall south of Nantucket Island, allowing it to concentrate its full strength just to the north, along coastal Massachusetts. Before the storm finally headed out to sea, its raging winds coupled with three feet of snow would claim ninety-nine lives.

After a quick breakfast, Frank did a little engine maintenance down in the underbelly of the *Can Do*, followed by some paperwork. About the time his work was finished, the wind began kicking up a considerable chop in the harbor. A few flakes of dry snow fell as Frank left the *Can Do* and walked to his car, pulling the collar of his jacket more snugly around his neck in the cold breeze. His coat was a gift from the Coast Guard Station Gloucester, an olive-green officer's jacket, which Frank wore with pride.

Frank hopped in his car and drove southwest on Rogers Street and Western Avenue, along the waterfront. He passed the Coast Guard station and the Fisherman's Memorial, where the names of hundreds of men lost at sea are etched in granite blocks. At the western end of Gloucester Harbor, he crossed the drawbridge that spans the narrow canal connecting the harbor to the Annisquam River. Then he turned right on Essex Avenue and pulled into the parking lot of the Cape Ann Marina, where a large American flag snapped overhead. Frank was greeted by his friend and marina vice president, Louis Linquata, who was not surprised to see him. Frank always wanted to be near his boat during foul weather and make himself available just in case the Coast Guard needed his services.

Linquata and Frank were joined by maintenance supervisor Gard Estes, and the three men fanned out to the marina's many docks to secure boats and equipment. A few people lived on their boats year-round, and as Gard tightened lines, he made sure no one intended to remain aboard a boat during the storm. The breeze died down briefly, and in the eerie calm Gard noticed he was being followed by three seagulls, walking on the dock just three feet behind him. When he stopped, they stopped, but as soon as he resumed walking, they stayed right at his heels. Usually the gulls gave people a wide berth, yet that day they followed Gard everywhere. He wondered if the birds knew something about the coming snow that he didn't.

When the men's work was done at one P.M., they went inside for lunch and a beer. The marina's restaurant and lounge were only a few years old, and the furnishings still looked new. One of Gard's friends had recently contributed his own personal touch, bringing in a six-foot-long Styrofoam bluefin tuna and hanging it on the back wall "to add a little more character." The restaurant and bar had become a cozy meeting place for Frank's wide circle of friends from Gloucester, including cops, carpenters, and fishermen.

Sitting down to a bowl of steaming chowder at the bar, Frank looked out the sliders and noticed how the wind had picked back up and was angrily stirring the black waters of the Annisquam River. The snow was still relatively light, but it was now being driven horizontally each time a particularly strong gust swept up the river from the ocean. During lunch the three men discussed the latest weather reports and learned that the snow was piling up in Providence, Rhode Island, ninety miles away. At this point it was still possible that the storm might swing out to sea and spare Gloucester. Their eyes told them otherwise: outside the sky was getting darker, and it looked more like dusk than midday.

Over the course of the afternoon, the men were joined by other friends: commercial fisherman Kenneth Fuller, thirty-four, of Rockport; Norman David Curley, thirty-five, a Gloucester electrician; and thirty-six-year-old Don Wilkinson of Rockport, who managed the Captain's Bounty Motor Lodge. The men were relaxed, eating chowder and sipping beer while shooting the breeze, glad for an early end to the workday because of the approaching storm. Being the only customers in the restaurant, they could be as noisy as they liked, and because they were all such good friends, they started teasing one another. Some of the men were standing around the bar; others, sitting and smoking cigarettes. Frank enjoyed himself as much as his friends, but he also had one ear glued to the radio, monitoring the news about the storm.

At midafternoon the group was joined by Bill Lee, an oil barge captain who filled commercial vessels with fuel. Lee knew all the men, as their paths frequently crossed either on the waterfront or in the harbor. He and Frank had a lot in common, as they were both Navy Seabees, and they saw each other almost every day while working. Sometimes Frank would be in the *Can Do* waiting to off-load a pilot and Lee would be right next to him in his barge waiting to fuel the ship. Lee considered Frank an excellent mariner.

Lee socialized with the other men at the marina, and he recalls how nobody called Curley by his real first name of Norman, because he went by his middle name, David. "He was a quiet guy," says Lee, "but he could be very funny. And he could take a joke, too: we always gave him the business about his bald head. He was at home on boats, because he had a twenty-four-foot cabin cruiser that he loved. He was always there to do a favor. Don Wilkinson was always talking about his two children and wife. His big thing was football, and I remember he went to the Super Bowl every year. Don also raced powerboats. He was the bookworm of the group as well, and very bright. At one time he ran the marina and later became its business manager."

Lee recalls Kenny Fuller as a street-smart guy who was constantly coming up with new ideas to make money. He was a free spirit who was always up for fun but willing to pitch in if work needed to get done. As a commercial fisherman who owned his own boat, he would go far offshore fishing for tuna in the summer and fall, and often ended the season by navigating his vessel from Gloucester to Florida.

When Lee joined the group at the marina that afternoon, he told Frank that while he was out fueling boats, he had heard that an oil tanker, the *Global Hope* in Salem Sound, was in a bit of trouble. Even though the tanker had its anchor set, the winds were pushing the vessel so hard it was slowly moving, dragging anchor down in Salem. The northeast winds had pushed the ship a few hundred feet to the southwest. "I realized," says Lee, "that was one of the ships Frank had brought in and figured he'd want to know. By this time it was snowing pretty hard, and the winds were getting stronger each hour."

The first people to notice that the *Global Hope* had shifted position were concerned residents along the Beverly waterfront. They called local police, who in turn notified Warren Andrews, the operator of the Salem Control radio station, which monitored all shipping in busy Salem Channel. Andrews had lost his sight at a young age but was a superb radio control operator, able to juggle all the incoming radio traffic and coordinate the activity. He always wore dark glasses and kept his graying hair combed straight back. His radio control room was off an L-shaped addition to his house.

Andrews grew up in Salem, and he could remember all the features of Salem Harbor from when he had his sight. Frank's son Frank III recalls several visits with his dad: "Andrews was amazing. He could move from one radio to the next in that control room in an instant. I marveled at his skill without the ability to see. I once said to my dad, 'Are you sure he's blind?' " Others compared Warren to an old lighthouse keeper, because he was always there.

Andrews made tape recordings of most of his daily radio activity, as a way to check facts at a later date if someone had a question he couldn't answer off the top of his head. That afternoon was no exception, and the tape chronicles how Andrews notified the nearest Coast Guard station (in Gloucester) when the first calls came in regarding the *Global Hope*.

Coast Guard Station Gloucester immediately made contact with the captain of the *Global Hope*, asking if he had noticed a position change in his vessel since he last anchored. The captain, who was Greek, had a strong accent, and sometimes he struggled for the right word in English.

Station Gloucester repeated the question: *"We need to verify if you have dragged anchor. Over."*

The *Global Hope* responded, *"No, nothing."*

"Roger that. We received a report that you did drag anchor. Are you in distress now? Is there any reason you would be in distress?"

"No, up to now, up to now, nothing, ship stay in this position. We are in same position, same position as anchored."

"Keep us informed, skipper, if you drag anchor any more."

"Okay, thank you."

From this exchange it seems the Coast Guard doubted the captain's ability to judge whether the *Global Hope* had dragged anchor or not. Their qualms were well founded.

After Bill Lee left the group to finish a final fueling job, Frank, Curley, Wilkinson, and Fuller paid their bill and headed down to the *Can Do* docked in the South Channel. Once on the boat, Frank called Andrews for the latest news on the *Global Hope*. Next, Frank radioed Coast Guard Station Gloucester, informing them that he was dockside and standing by on channels 16 and 12. The Coast Guard men and women at Station Gloucester all knew Frank and were aware that he could be counted on should they need his services. Several times he had assisted on rescues and also conducted dives for the Coast Guard, often helping commercial fishing boat draggers free their nets from submerged debris.

The group of men sat around a table in the *Can Do*'s wheel-house, directly behind the captain's chair and wheel. Visitors to the *Can Do*'s wheelhouse, surrounded with thick aluminum, compared it to a tank with windows. Everything about the boat was solid, prompting one mariner to call it a "fortress," while another described it as a "surface submarine." The *Can Do* was bobbing next to the dock, but the hissing of the wind was muffled by the thick superstructure, and the men could carry on conversations as normal. They monitored the radio and realized wind gusts were approaching hurricane force.

On board the *Can Do*, the men were quite comfortable. The forty-nine-foot boat originally had been the pleasure yacht of a wealthy family from Rhode Island. Frank had bought the boat because it was built to take a beating, with a three-eighths-inch steel hull and a quarter-inch aluminum pilothouse. Frank modified the boat for his piloting, adding such features as a rubber bumper at the tip of the bow, and installing fat racing tires on the sides for protection when the *Can Do* was brought alongside tankers and freighters. In addition, he had installed an array of electronics for communication and guidance: two FM radios, two CB radios, a ship-to-shore AM radio, a loran (long range electronic navigation device) for land coordinates, top quality radar, and huge searchlights.

The *Can Do* also had all the luxuries of home. A spiral staircase with a stainless steel railing and mahogany steps led from the pilothouse forward to the "mates' quarters," which had two bunks, mahogany drawers beneath each bunk, a retractable television, a sink, and a toilet. From these quarters there was access to a storage compartment in the bow where anchorage material was stowed. In the aft section were the captain's quarters and the galley. Four people could sleep in the captain's quarters, which featured a walk-in closet, carpeted floor, mahogany woodwork throughout, large eighteen-by-eight-inch portholes that opened, and a toilet, sink, and shower. A full-size refrigerator, sink, counters, gas range, and stove made up the galley. Amidships, between the captain's and mates' quarters, was the engine room, where a Cummins 220-horsepower engine turned the large single propeller that powered the boat through the seas.

When Frank piloted the boat, he literally had everything at his fingertips: steering wheel, stainless steel compass, chrome navigational controls, access to all the radios, drawers for the charts and logbooks, controls for the searchlights, and a long wooden handle suspended from a chain for the whistle. Just behind the captain's controls was the large mahogany table with cushioned benches where the men now sat shooting the breeze and, like many others in Massachusetts, wondering if this blizzard would be as bad as the one that had struck just three weeks earlier. That blizzard had set a record for snowfall but caused little damage, and seaside communities weathered it in stride.

At about four thirty, Bill Lee finished his last fueling job, anchored his barge, and then checked on his pleasure boat in a slip within a stone's throw of the *Can Do* before rejoining his friends. The men were listening to the marine radio for more information about the *Global Hope*. There were no further transmissions between the Coast Guard and the ship, however, and they assumed the tanker was holding position and in good shape. They had no idea just how quickly the storm was turning into a monster.

"We knew it was bad out there," says Lee, "but nobody had any idea how awful it was beyond the breakwater. Frank was talking about maybe going down to Salem so he could have his boat on hand in the morning, knowing a pilot or shipping agent would want to be brought to the *Global Hope*."

About five P.M., Lee figured his wife might wonder where he was and headed home. Just after he left, the men still on board heard a frantic, crackling distress cry on the radio.

"Coast Guard, Coast Guard, this is Global Hope*!"*

"This is Coast Guard Station Gloucester."

"We are in dangerous place! The water is coming inside into engine!"

"Did you say you are taking on water?"

"Water in engine room, engine room! Hull is broken!"

"Did you say the hull is broken and you are taking on water in the engine room?"

"Yes, that's correct."

"We will dispatch a boat with a pump at this time; stand by."

Station Gloucester immediately contacted Boston Search and Rescue, which dispatched the ninety-five-foot cutter *Cape George*. Search and Rescue also instructed a much larger cutter, the 210-foot *Decisive*, to leave its anchorage outside Provincetown, Cape Cod, and speed to Salem. Boston, however, is about twenty-five nautical miles from Salem, and Provincetown is fifty. With sixty-knot winds blowing, they might not get to the crippled tanker in time.

Station Gloucester next radioed Andrews at Salem Control, hoping against the odds that there would be a boat in Salem that could aid the *Global Hope*. Warren said there were no boats available at this time of year.

This was what Station Gloucester had feared. With Salem fifteen nautical miles from Gloucester and the storm building by the minute, Station Gloucester was faced with a terrible choice. The only boats at their disposal were two relatively small patrol boats, one a forty-one-footer and the other a forty-four-footer. On the one hand, to send them into the storm, which by then had whipped the ocean's surface into ten-foot seas, was dangerous. On the other hand, there were thirty-two men aboard the *Global Hope* whose lives were in jeopardy.

Frank had been monitoring the nervous exchanges on the radio and broke in: *"There's nothing we can do at this end, either, at this time, but we will be standing by still dockside at Gloucester. I want you to be aware that as far as I know, the ship is about six hundred and eighty feet long, and she is light, very light* [most of the cargo of oil had been off-loaded], *and the last I got she is about eleven foot forward and twenty foot aft* [below the waterline], *and whether they ballast* [add seawater to special tanks designed to provide stability when they're filled] *it down after that or not, I don't know. And it is going to be one great big problem if they do have a problem due to conditions here."*

Station Gloucester responded: *"Roger that; I think I'm going to get a boat under way, and give him* [the *Global Hope* captain] *a call to see how bad he is taking on water."*

Frank urged caution and also said he would be on the *Can Do* in case they were needed to help. He then made a call to Charlie Bucko, who at twenty-nine had recently left the Coast Guard to take a job repairing boats at the Gloucester Marine Railway. Charlie and Frank were the best of friends, and because of Charlie's Coast Guard training and rescue missions, he had plenty of experience in stormy seas. He was living with his fiancée, Sharon Watts, on Eastern Point Road in Gloucester not far from the *Can Do*.

"We had just finished dinner," says Sharon, "when Frank called. He said there was a tanker in trouble in Salem, and he wanted Charlie on board in case they needed to go down and help. Charlie said he'd be right over. By this time it was snowing really hard, and I could hear the winds howling outside. He knew I was concerned, and he said, 'Don't worry; it was just as bad during the *Chester Poling*, and I made it back, so I'll make it back from this.' Then he gave me a big hug and said, 'I love you.'" The *Chester Poling* was a tanker that had been wrecked the previous year, and Charlie had helped to rescue the crew.

Bill Lee was also a friend of Charlie's and recalls that when Charlie was a coxswain in the Coast Guard, the younger men looked up to him because he was confident, outspoken, and had been decorated for bravery twice while fighting in the Vietnam War. But he also had a soft side, like the time he found an injured seagull. The seagull had a broken wing, and Charlie felt sorry for it. Somehow he was able to get his hands around the injured gull and bring it back to Station Gloucester. Then he built a little pen for it out back, and every day Charlie tended to the gull, feeding it fish and making sure it was healthy before releasing it.

When Charlie reached the *Can Do*, the situation with the *Global Hope* had become more confusing because communication with the tanker had suddenly ceased, presumably from water shorting out its power. Station Gloucester had no way of knowing if the ship was sinking, breaking apart, or not in any immediate danger. It was ink-black outside, with blinding snow, and no one down in Salem could see the *Global Hope*.

Station Gloucester made the difficult decision to send both patrol boats down to Salem, probably thinking with two boats together, one could help the other if they encountered trouble on the way.

THE COAST GUARD
RESPONDS

The two patrol boats that Station Gloucester dispatched to the *Global Hope* were usually sufficient for rescue operations along Boston's North Shore. The forty-one-footer, #41353, was a utility boat whose primary duties were boarding, firefighting, law enforcement, and search and rescue in seas up to seven or eight feet. Its sleeker, lighter design made it considerably faster than the forty-four-footer but not nearly as tough. The Forty-Four, #44317, was a motor lifeboat also used for patrols and search and rescue, but it sacrificed speed for seaworthiness in heavy weather. First built in the 1960s, the vessel had eight watertight compartments, twin diesel engines, a heavy steel hull, and a concrete-weighted keel. If the twenty-ton forty-four-footer rolled over, it could right itself. The righting process, however, could take up to thirty seconds—which would have seemed like an eternity to anyone on board.

The cutter classification is reserved for Coast Guard vessels sixty-five feet in length or greater with adequate accommodations for the crew to live on board. While Station Gloucester did not and does not have a cutter of its own, cutters often dock in Gloucester for two-week periods between patrols. Unfortunately, during the Blizzard of '78, the region's ninety-five-foot cutters, the *Cape George* and the *Cape Cross*, were berthed in Boston, and the larger *Decisive* was even farther away, at Provincetown, Cape Cod.

Every Coast Guard man or woman seems to have his or her own special preference for the type of vessel to be assigned to. However, one common theme expressed has more to do with the length of time at sea rather than the vessel itself. "I couldn't stand those cutters," says a thirty-year veteran of the Coast Guard. "If you were out in sloppy weather and you were seasick, it was pure hell, because the cutters stayed out so long. I'd be puking for five days straight, not caring if they threw me overboard. At least with the forty-fours, you know there's an end in sight. Once the mission was accomplished, we went back to port, since there are no sleeping accommodations on board. I don't even like to hear the term *ninety-five-footer*. I was on one for a short while, and I vowed never again."

Some rookies in the Coast Guard think that the larger the boat, the safer you are, but this is not necessarily the case, since the cutters stay out in nastier weather. An example of what can happen to a large cutter in harm's way was the *LV 73*, a 123-foot, 693-ton vessel that was stationed at Vineyard Sound, Massachusetts. The ship sank off the Martha's Vineyard coast during the Hurricane of 1944, and all twelve hands on board were lost. One hundred and twenty-three feet isn't much compared to the brute force of hurricane-whipped seas.

While Coast Guard vessels are not indestructible, they are always shipshape and well maintained. The floundering *Global Hope*, however, was reported to be neither. After Frank Quirk had delivered the pilot to the vessel, and the man had guided the tanker through Salem's narrow shipping channel into port, the *Global Hope* had proceeded to unload its fuel. Most of the oil had been off-loaded when a worker noticed that water had mixed with the fuel, possibly from a broken water line or heating coil used to keep the fuel at an optimal temperature for discharge. When this was discovered, the tanker was ordered to move away from the terminal and drop anchor outside the harbor. Some accounts also reported the ship had inadequate fire protection— yet another reason to move it away from the terminal. The Salem harbormaster referred to the tanker as "an old ship, built about twenty-eight years ago and not in very good shape."

Approximately two hundred thousand gallons of oil were still on board, and the plan was to let the fuel solidify so that the water could then be pumped off. Once the water was removed, the tanker could return to the terminal and finish off-loading the fuel. The blizzard, however, would scratch that plan.

With a potential disaster in the making, Chief Warrant Officer Edmund "Mike" Paradis, the commanding officer of Station Gloucester, now felt compelled to take charge of the radio and direct the operation personally. At some stations, the commanding officer is close to his men, socializing a bit and getting to know the crew personally. Paradis, however, kept a strict chain of command. He was described by the men he led as "aloof" and "by the book."

Paradis was in his late forties, tall and fit, with hair that had gone prematurely white. Usually he had a pipe in his mouth, occasionally sending up a puff of smoke from a stern and unsmiling mouth. In the mess hall he had his own section partitioned off from the rest of the men, and his table was the only one with linen. You joined him by invitation only. Men who served under him describe him as all business, a real no-nonsense kind of guy whom no one wanted to cross. He treated the station like an underway ship and almost never dealt directly with the younger Coasties who did not report directly to him. Despite his distant, reserved nature, he was proud of his crew, and they in turn respected his competence.

~

Paradis and Frank knew and trusted each other, often discussing the latest Coast Guard news. Although their personalities were quite different, they had a common bond by virtue of being older than all the other servicemen. Station Gloucester was just a couple of wharves away from the *Can Do*'s slip, and Frank swung by the station for coffee almost as frequently as off-duty Coasties dropped in on Frank. The station, a nondescript three-story brick building, is right on the waterfront, with a helicopter pad and a pier for the patrol boats. Inside is a radio room, an equipment room, a cafeteria that seats about thirty, and sleeping quarters. Men stationed there say they can wake up and not even look out the window to know when the seas are rough because the water in the toilet bowls sloshes around. On this day in 1978, the toilet bowl water was really hopping.

When word first reached Paradis that the *Global Hope* was taking on water, his primary concern was for the welfare of the crew. However, it's probable he was also thinking about the cargo of oil, especially in light of the *Argo Merchant* disaster, which had occurred a little over a year earlier. The *Argo Merchant* was a 29,870-ton Liberian-registered oil tanker, approximately the same length as the *Global Hope*. It, too, ran hard aground and took on water in the engine room, although the *Argo Merchant* did not meet its demise by dragging anchor but instead through the poor navigation of its captain, who led the ship directly into a treacherous patch of shoals south of Nantucket Island, Massachusetts. The crew was rescued by the Coast Guard, and every effort was made to free the tanker from the shoal, but the incessant pounding of the seas caused the hull to break apart, sending more than seven and a half million gallons of oil spreading over the ocean.

Paradis knew the *Global Hope* had off-loaded some of its cargo, but the ship was only a mile or two from shore. An oil spill there would be a calamity. The black goo would cover pristine beaches and important fishing grounds, fouling not only the coast and the marine environment but the local economy as well. If his men could make it to the tanker and stabilize the situation by getting pumps on board, perhaps the tanker could hold together until the larger cutters arrived.

Paradis had approved the dispatching of the forty-one- and forty-four-footers, and now as the boats set off, he took over the radio, sitting down before a broad array of communications equipment. A window looked out upon the harbor. Although Paradis could see nothing in the black void, he heard the wind howling, and when a particularly strong gust pummeled the building, he hoped the window wouldn't break.

In the interior of the room, next to the entry door, a large glass panel separated the room from a main hallway. Curious Coasties stole glances at the chief, concerned about their station mates now out in the blizzard. Their concern was well founded, because as the Forty-One and Forty-Four reached the opening of Gloucester Harbor, they were slammed by raging seas and a screeching wind coming out of the northeast.

The skipper of the Forty-One thought the boat might flip, and near the breakwater by Round Rock Shoal, he radioed Paradis that they were heading back in. *"Taking quite a beating,"* the skipper shouted over the howling wind. *"Seven-footers out here, breaking, too. We are taking them solid right over the bow."*

Now it would be up to the Forty-Four and its crew: seamen Robert Krom and Roger Mathurin, engineer Tom Desrosiers, and skipper/coxswain Bob McIlvride. All four were young, from nineteen to twenty-three, and this was the first time they had been teamed on a mission. As soon as the Forty-Four exited Gloucester Harbor, they had problems with their radar, fathometer (used to measure water depth), and FM radio, probably due to icing and the size of the seas. They used the vessel's spotty radar along with the compass to navigate.

McIlvride was tall and thin, with blond hair and a baby face that made him look like he was sixteen rather than twenty-one. He was described by crew members as extremely bright yet low-key and unassuming—the perfect kind of coxswain in a situation like the blizzard. As the Forty-Four left the safety of Gloucester Harbor, even the soft-spoken McIlvride had tension in his voice as he shouted to be heard over the canvas curtains cracking in the wind. He had been on search-and-rescue missions before, but never in seas like this, and he gripped the wheel until his knuckles were white. He also got soaked with icy spray as a particularly strong gust blew away a section of the canvas curtain.

The windshield was covered in ice and snow, and McIlvride had to rely on his crew to help him search for buoys in the blackness. All four of the men were standing in the pilothouse, hanging on as best they could, taking turns watching the faltering radar and peering through blinding snow for buoys. The light on the compass went out, and they had to shine flashlights on the needle to get a directional fix. Heading southwest toward Salem, they were going in the same direction as the waves, and each one catapulted the boat ahead.

Desrosiers, the boat's engineer, remembers that the waves were so large—approximately fifteen to twenty feet—that when they were in the troughs of the waves, they couldn't see a thing. Then, each time they crested a wave, the men would anxiously search for the flashing lights of buoys in near whiteout conditions. One enormous channel buoy nearly killed the men just a few minutes into their mission. They never saw it until the buoy rode up a wave and was directly above the boat. Desrosiers shouted, "Turn! Turn!" Bob McIlvride turned first to port, then quickly to starboard, to clear the stern, and the buoy just missed smashing the Forty-Four before it crashed back into the sea. Had it hit the boat, it might have caused it to capsize, and if it had hit a crewman, it would have crushed him like a bug. As the buoy receded to stern, McIlvride said, "Well, I guess we found that one."

"I was glad Bob was piloting the boat," Desrosiers recalls. "Even though he was as young as the rest of us, he had a mind like a vise and knew exactly where those aids [buoys] were supposed to be from all his time studying charts."

Seaman Bob Krom has similar praise for the coxswain: "I had a lot of confidence in McIlvride; the tone of his voice showed he was in control of himself. Sea conditions were so bad, though, I must admit I wondered if we were going to make it. It's pitch-black, and we could only see the breaking waves at the last second; then a wall of white water would crash on the stern. I was thinking, *How on earth does this boat stay afloat?* If we rolled, the only thing we could do was take a quick bite of air and hold on."

McIlvride couldn't see out the windshield, as it was iced and covered with snow: "The front windshield was in three panels. The middle panel, right in front of the wheel, was fixed in place, but the ones on either side could be opened. I had the crew open those two and keep a sharp lookout for the buoys. Because we were going with the seas and the wind was at our back, we didn't take much water through these openings—all the water was coming over the stern and the sides.

"I never thought about turning back, and my objective was to find the light at Baker's Island. The only safe way to enter Salem Sound is through the gap between Baker's and Misery Island—if you go north or south of those islands, it's all shoals. So I figured if we could just find Baker's and keep it on our port side, we'd at least get into Salem Sound. I was way too busy to be afraid. It was probably tougher for the other guys because they had time to think—and to pray. I kept thinking about the tanker and wondering what the heck we were supposed to do once we found it."

McIlvride had had a somewhat unusual boyhood. His father was a minister who was assigned to Thailand, where Bob spent seven years of his boyhood. When he was in the States, he spent summers on his uncle's thirty-foot Chris-Craft, and that's how Bob learned boat handling and deepened his attachment to water. After graduating from high school, he attended Penn State and was a member of the sailing team. During his second year, the team was participating in meets in Chesapeake Bay, and

McIlvride watched the Coast Guard boats cruising the bay. As he observed the men on the boats, it dawned on him that that was what he wanted to do with his life.

He considered that very moment the first time he really took control of his life, and he made the decision to leave school and join up. McIlvride had always dreamed of being in the Coast Guard but never really acted on it until then. At home he had a Coast Guard poster on the door of his bedroom. The picture on the poster was of a patrol boat crashing through a huge wave. The boat on the poster was a forty-four.

Once McIlvride joined, he made it his objective to become a coxswain of a forty-four. He found boot camp to be a grueling ordeal. But once he realized he could survive it, he felt his self-confidence grow. Friends and relatives who saw him after he completed boot camp told him he'd changed, and he had. He had a newfound confidence that made him feel he could do anything he put his mind to. Out of a boot camp group of about seventy young men, McIlvride graduated number two. With the high ranking came the opportunity to pick his "billet," his first duty station. Out of anywhere in the country, McIlvride chose Group Boston, because they had search-and-rescue operations on small boats, including the Forty-Four. Friends said he was crazy—why didn't he pick Hawaii, Florida, or California?—but McIlvride knew he'd made the right choice.

On the one hand, McIlvride was a typical young Coastie, gung ho and ready to tackle any mission, but he also had an unconventional streak. He was friendly with his fellow servicemen at Gloucester, but he also spent a fair amount of time alone, rarely joining in the off-duty drinking and partying. In fact, he used some of his free time to learn and practice Transcendental Meditation, often sitting in the upper stairwell landing of the three-story station to find solitude and meditate.

While at Station Gloucester he did whatever he could to reach his goal of becoming a coxswain on a forty-four. Whenever he had radio watch, which was usually very slow, he spent much of the time studying the charts in the communications room. (This was long before the advent of GPS.) He focused on the chart that covered an area from Marblehead to the north side of Rockport. McIlvride studied that chart so diligently he had it memorized, which was a blessing the night of the blizzard—there was no way charts could be read on the open bridge.

He reached his goal of the coxswain designation in January 1978, just one month before the blizzard struck.

~

Despite the pounding Bob McIlvride, Tom Desrosiers, Roger Mathurin, and Bob Krom were taking, they battled their way south. At 6:45 P.M., they radioed that they were one-third of the way to Baker's Island, which is located at the mouth of Salem Sound. But a few minutes later, Andrews radioed that he was getting reports from people who had been hearing a ship's whistle continually blowing short blasts, indicating distress. The men on the Forty-Four assumed that the whistle was from the tanker, and they wondered if they would find the ship in pieces, with sailors in the water.

Back in Gloucester Harbor, Frank was growing more concerned about the Forty-Four as he monitored the radio and heard their mounting problems. He knew each of the young men on the Forty-Four, and it's likely that because they were about the same age as Frank's oldest son, he was as worried as a father would be. They might have been Coast Guard trained, but the combined maritime experience of the four was still less than his own days at sea. By this time, he and the four other men aboard the *Can Do* had discussed the risks involved in going out into a storm that showed no signs of weakening. Charlie Bucko, being a former Coast Guard coxswain, had committed himself to staying on board with Frank, but Frank tried to dissuade the others from making the trip to Salem Sound.

Fifteen-year-old Mark Gelinas, a friend of Frank's younger son, Brian, had trudged down to the *Can Do* that evening. "I wanted to go out with the men," recalls Gelinas, "but of course Frank said no way. Frank also told Wilkinson, Fuller, and Curley not to go. He said it was going to be awful out there and that, once they got to Salem, he wasn't going to come back that night, and he wasn't sure when he and Bucko would be back."

Each man wanted to help, knowing they would be needed if they had to pluck men from the Forty-Four or the tanker out of heavy seas, and they elected to accompany Frank and Charlie. Maybe the group dynamics made it hard for one person to leave when all the others were prepared to go. No one wanted to appear afraid. On the other hand, the men had so much experience at sea that they never would have taken the conditions lightly. They knew that once the *Can Do* was beyond the breakwater, they would be on their own, in an unpredictable situation where the unforeseen could mean disaster. If they got into trouble, there were no other Coast Guard boats in Gloucester that could help them.

~

Somehow Charlie managed to run to a phone and call Sharon before they headed out. He simply said, "We'll be heading out soon. I love you." On the surface, this might seem an odd thing to do, because just thirty minutes earlier he had said goodbye to Sharon and told her he loved her.

Whether Charlie had a premonition or just a sense of foreboding, the phone call to Sharon showed his concern. He knew the risks of going out in such a storm. But with mariners on the *Global Hope* in trouble and the men on the Forty-Four potentially in need of help, it would have been virtually impossible for him not to try to aid fellow mariners. He had the Coast Guard mentality of helping those in need as well as the marine mind-set of leaving no man behind. Going out to help was part of who Charlie was, and taking action was instinctive.

~

Frank radioed Paradis for an update and let him know his intentions. *"What's the status of the Forty-Four? How are they making out?"*

"She's about one-third of the way down there. We had to turn the Forty-One back."

"Let's wait a few more minutes. In about another fifteen minutes, I may give it a shot. We'll give it a try to get over there."

"What do you have for crew?"

"I've got Bucko here and a couple of hands."

"Pat wants you to give him a shout if you want another man. He would be glad to go with you."

In this exchange it's clear that, although Frank was willing to "give it a try," if the conditions proved too much for the *Can Do*, he would turn back. The men aboard figured there was no harm in seeing what it was like outside the harbor, believing they had the option of turning back. Both literally and figuratively, they wanted to test the waters and see how the *Can Do* responded—after all, Frank's boat was forty-nine feet, a bit larger than the Forty-Four. To sit in the harbor and do nothing while four young Coast Guard men were out there alone in increasing danger was unacceptable to all five men.

While Frank prepared to head into the blizzard, the ninety-five-foot Coast Guard cutter *Cape George* left port in Boston and began the journey to the *Global Hope*. The cutter's home port was Falmouth, Massachusetts, but on that day, the ship was moored in Boston after a patrol. Aboard the cutter was Executive Petty Officer Myron Verville, who recalls that the seas grew with each passing mile as the *Cape George* made its way to the tanker. The cutter's fathometer went out near Logan Airport, and when it approached Governor's Island, the seas were six feet, with winds at forty-five knots. Verville knew things were going to be bad, because these heavy seas were still in the shelter of Boston Harbor.

Once the cutter got past Governor's Island and headed to port (northeast) toward Salem, they were pounded by chaotic seas greater than twenty feet. Verville had never seen salt water freeze so fast, and the entire boat was soon covered and weighted down with ice, significantly slowing its progress. The ice on the boat weighed an estimated forty tons, and Verville was worried about all that extra weight. It not only affected their speed but also was a real danger to the vessel's stability, especially when it built up well above the waterline.

Normally the *Cape George* could make a run from Boston to Salem in under two hours, but because they were going into the teeth of the wind and were slowed by the weight of ice, each mile gained was taking four times longer than normal.

The Forty-Four, however, was racing with the seas, like a toy boat propelled down a raging river. At seven P.M. they reached Baker's Island in Salem Sound with frayed nerves as the storm exploded into its full fury.

"With the searchlights on," says Roger Mathurin, "all we could see was snow coming down almost horizontally and enormous seas. Let me give you an idea of how bad it was. The top of our radar antenna extended exactly thirteen feet, three inches, above the waterline. When we were down in the troughs, I could look up and see a wall of water that was about fifteen feet above the top of the antenna. When we were down in those troughs, it was eerily quiet. The wind didn't reach down there, but as soon as we rode up the next wave, there was incredible shrieking from the wind. I've been in the Coast Guard twenty-five years, and I've never seen seas that were anything like those."

Just before reaching Baker's Island, the Forty-Four was clobbered by an enormous wave. The wall of water put the vessel on its side, its antenna masts in the ocean. For a harrowing split second, it seemed the boat would keep rolling and capsize. Instead, it quickly came back up and McIlvride regained control. Although the Forty-Four was designed to right itself from a roll, the crew would have been swept off. None of them had strapped themselves in with surf belts, because they needed to be able to move quickly and be searching for navigation aids. Even after the near capsizing, there was no way they could locate the crude harnesses and get them on in the wildly pitching boat.

Paradis told McIlvride to be very careful approaching the tanker, because it had a black hull and white superstructure and was probably not showing any lights whatsoever. McIlvride asked for a more accurate position for the *Global Hope*. Paradis didn't know for sure.

McIlvride was coaxing the boat onward like a jockey atop a Thoroughbred horse running full speed on a slippery track. One false step and down they'd go. *Just a little more,* he thought. *Just a little farther.* But his mount was slowly succumbing to the brutal pounding. He and his crew struggled with a radar system that had completely shut down. They could have been four feet from slamming into the *Global Hope* and not even known it. Even if the crew could locate the tanker, there was little they could do. This was the moment all four crewmen realized they might perish. They were in grave danger without radar, and the storm was still strengthening.

The storm had also taken its toll on other equipment on the Forty-Four; the fathometer was broken. Not only did the crew not know what was in front of the boat, but they also didn't know what was below them—they could be in fifty feet of water or five feet. (The Forty-Four's hull extended 3.5 feet below the surface.) This was particularly troublesome because both inside and outside Salem Sound there were shoals and shallow ledges. The next wave might hurl the boat into a foaming mess of water swirling around submerged rocks. If that happened, they could have their propeller flattened or their hull split. If the hit was sudden enough, the boat would lurch to a stop and the next wave would push it broadside, leaving it vulnerable to capsizing.

Navigation around Baker's Island does not allow much room for error. To the south are Pope Head Shoal, North Gooseberry Island, South Gooseberry Island, and the ominous-sounding Dry Breakers. Aptly named Misery Shoal and Misery Island, where more than one mariner has met his end, are to the north. Between Misery Island and Baker's Island is a thousand-yard passage. Then it's four miles through Salem Sound to the ports of Salem and Beverly, but scattered through the region are more islands and submerged ledges. Nautical charts of Salem Sound show depth contour lines in crazy, haphazard patterns where it might be twenty feet on one side of the boat and four feet on the other.

Navigating through Salem Sound blind, without radar or visibility, would be like trying to run raging rapids at night in a kayak.

When Paradis realized the radar and fathometer on the Forty-Four were out for good and his men didn't know exactly where they were, his concern tripled. The topography of the ocean's floor around Baker's Island resembles the craggy spine of a ridge with a mix of level areas, swales, and sharply rising peaks. It was the peaks he was most worried about. They are the submerged granite humps that, along with the sandy shoals, litter outer Salem Sound. Those ledges can grab a boat and crumple a steel hull as if it were made of aluminum foil.

Paradis knew he had to get the men on board the Forty-Four to safety and barked into the microphone, *"The moment you can identify a floating aid, any known aid, and you can work your way into Beverly, do so immediately."*

McIlvride acknowledged the instructions, and Paradis told him to forget about the tanker. At this point getting the Forty-Four to safety was the priority.

Proceeding to Beverly, however, was easier said than done. Even though the Forty-Four was just four miles from the docks at Beverly, the crew was disoriented without functioning radar, wondering if the next wave would thrust them into rocks. The men half expected to hear the sickening noise of their hull grinding on a shoal or, even worse, the crash of their bow into a ledge.

Paradis radioed Frank to resume their discussion and described what he'd decided about the Forty-Four. There was uncertainty in the comments of both men, who seemed to be groping to make the right decision:

Paradis: *"If I can get that boat back to safe water, that's what I'm going to do. Do you figure on going up there?"*

Frank: *"Well, we'll take a shot at it. I don't know. And if I do get up there, I kinda know the area a little bit, for what it's worth. I don't know; it's going to be one hell of a mess from here."*

Paradis: *"Roger. At this time, we don't know for sure whether anybody is in fact in jeopardy. We know there is a probability the ship is dragging her anchor. We have other Coast Guard facilities coming on the scene, a two-ten and a ninety-five. I don't see any reason for jeopardizing a small boat crew that doesn't have the facilities at their disposal."*

Frank: *"Roger on that. Well, with your okay, I'd like to take a look outside the harbor and see about heading up that way or whether I stay here."*

Paradis: *"Roger. Proceed outside, Frank, and give it a look. I appreciate it."*

Frank: *"Okay, we'll give it a look. The way it looks, we might be right back."*

FRANK QUIRK AND
CHARLIE BUCKO

Normally, the Coast Guard does not have frequent communication with a pilot boat captain, but Frank's many years of cooperation and assistance put him in a unique class. Quirk seemed to know how to make himself and the *Can Do* available to Station Gloucester without interfering or stepping on any toes. When dangerous situations occurred and Quirk was in the vicinity, he simply let the Coast Guard know he was standing by should they need him, often saying, "This is the *Can Do*; let me know if there's anything we can do to help."

Sometimes the Coast Guard took him up on his offer, and other times, when they had adequate vessels and personnel available, they didn't. And on rare occasions, there was no time for a discussion and immediate action was called for. One such incident involved a ten-year-old boy, Michael Almeida, who fell into Gloucester Harbor on an August afternoon in 1974.

Frank; his wife, Audrey; and their younger son, Brian, were aboard the *Can Do* in the process of towing the refrigerator ship *Reefer Merchant* into Gloucester. It was late in the day, about five thirty P.M., when Brian shouted, "Someone's in the water!"

Frank looked over to where Brian was pointing and saw a body floating about twenty feet from the end of the state pier. He immediately contacted the captain of the *Reefer Merchant* and told him to proceed on his own. Gunning the engine, Frank steered the *Can Do* toward the body and then handed over control of the boat to Audrey. Just a few feet from the scene, Frank lost sight of the body but then noticed a pair of fingertips barely breaking the water's surface. He also noticed a second person struggling in the water next to the pier. Grabbing a life ring, Frank ran to the stern of the *Can Do* and dived in.

Gloucester Harbor was quite murky, with all manner of foreign matter—including fish entrails from the nearby processing plant—suspended in the waters of the busy port. Swimming through the cloudy gray-green sea, Frank reached the submerged body. He made a grab for the hair on its head, but because of the oil and grease in the harbor, he could not sustain a grip. He took a big gulp of air and dived below. He grabbed the victim around the chest and started kicking for the pier, now aware that the body was that of a young boy who showed no signs of life.

A thirty-foot Coast Guard patrol boat roared toward the pier, and two seamen on board jumped over the side and helped Frank haul the boy the remaining feet to the pier. The skipper of the boat, Fiora Metall, maneuvered the boat to the dock and then assisted the men in the water. Together they raised the boy to the top of the pier, where Metall immediately began giving mouth-to-mouth resuscitation.

Meanwhile the person who had been struggling in the water, Fred Delourchry, made it back to the pier with the help of the seamen and collapsed. Delourchry had been sitting on the pier reading a book when the boy passed him on a bicycle, riding to the end of the pier.

"I looked up," said Delourchry in a police affidavit, "and noticed that he was no longer there. I jumped, looked around, and saw him in the water. At that point the bicycle that he was riding was dragging him down. I dove into the water and saw the bicycle was attached to his pant leg. He was five feet underwater about ten feet to the side of the pier. I shook the bicycle loose, and as I came up from under water, I struck my head on a camel [a floating pole at water level] that was adjacent to the pier. I was either unconscious or semiconscious." Delourchry said there was a gap in his memory, because the next thing he knew, he was on his back talking with Audrey Quirk on the pier.

Young Almeida was rushed to a local hospital, but his condition was so critical he was immediately moved to Boston's Children Hospital. Besides having his lungs filled with water from his ten to fifteen minutes under the surface, his condition was exacerbated by bacteria ingested from the pollution. Fortunately, after a lengthy stay in the hospital, he made a full recovery. Frank Quirk and Fred Delourchry both received Gloucester's Mariner's Medal for helping to save the boy's life. One of the nice things that came out of the accident was the close friendship that developed between the two rescuers. Almost every weekend in good weather, Delourchry would drive up from his Wellesley home and hang out on the *Can Do*. And Michael Almeida's parents didn't forget, either: they sent Michael's school picture to Frank for several years with a big thank-you note.

Warren Andrews says the rescue was typical Frank—"but there were other times, maybe less dramatic, that Frank also saved people from death or injury, and no one but Audrey and I knew about it." Warren points out that while Frank would do whatever he could to help those in need, including lending money to down-and-out fishermen, there was a tougher, no-nonsense side to him as well. Andrews recalls one incident in particular: "He once took two German officers from the hospital ship SS *Poseidon* to a local Gloucester restaurant for dinner. Two fishermen were there, and they became abusive to the German officers. Frank went over and asked them to cool it. One of the fishermen gave Frank a shove. Before you could bat an eyelash, that guy was on the floor clutching his stomach and the other was on his knees 'cause Frank had him in a hammerlock. It was all done so smoothly and quickly, most of the customers in the restaurant never even knew about the fight."

~

In many respects Frank and Charlie Bucko were quite similar. Charlie also went out of his way to help others—and other creatures, like the seagull—but he could be tough as nails, too. A former U.S. Marine, decorated in Vietnam with two Purple Hearts for combat wounds, Charlie had seen the crap life can throw at you—from the horrors of war to thirty-foot seas. He was big and burly but handsome, with blue eyes, a perfect smile, and long dark brown hair. Known as a first-rate boatswain's mate and an excellent boat handler, he was seen by other Coasties as a true leader.

Charlie seemed born for adventure. As early as eight years of age he found a neighbor trapped under a car that had fallen off a jack and ran and told his mother, who called the police. When he was eleven, a similar thing happened when a neighbor fell asleep while smoking and a small fire ignited inside the house. Charlie happened to notice smoke coming out of a window and pounded on the door, waking up the neighbor and potentially saving her life. When he was thirteen years old, he made his first full-blown rescue. Charlie's sister Janice recollected how he had been skating on a pond when another boy fell through the ice and disappeared. Charlie went in after the boy and dragged him up, saving his life. That night the boy's parents came over to the house to thank Charlie, and Janice, just seven years old at the time, listened in on the conversation, amazed to learn how Charlie went under the ice and didn't come up until he had found the boy.

Charlie Bucko's toughness was forged and tested in Vietnam. Janice remembers that the first time he was wounded, two marines came to her parents' house, and she thought for sure they were going to say he was dead. Instead they said Charlie had been wounded in the arm, but that they thought he would make a full recovery. The marine representatives brought the Buckos a Western Union telegram that stated Charlie had "sustained a gunshot wound to the left elbow from hostile rifle fire while on an operation." He had been in Vietnam for all of one month.

Charlie's arm did heal, but just a month later, his other arm was hit, this time by shrapnel during a firefight at Quang Tri Province. He was airlifted to the aircraft carrier *Valley Forge* for treatment and later sent to a hospital for further recovery. After his arm healed, he was stationed at Marine Headquarters in Okinawa, and upon completion of his duty there, he received an honorable discharge.

"When Charlie was released from the marines," says Janice, "he took the train back to New London. I remember it was winter and I was walking home from school and Charlie came trudging through the snowy streets. I ran over and hugged him and then we quietly walked the rest of the way home together as if it was just a regular day."

Once settled back in the U.S., Charlie took a few college courses but grew restless and started traveling, experiencing all he could. In New York City he took acting classes and did some theater only to pack up and move again after a few months. He wound up working on a cattle ranch in Idaho for a few more months, then pushed farther west to Seattle, where Janice was living at the time: "Charlie just blew into Seattle and spent several weeks with me. He was just so full of life, and he had the attitude of not sweating the small stuff. In fact, while he was living with me, I cracked up his car, and it was a total loss. He said, 'No big deal. You're okay, and that's all that matters.' "

~

Charlie had an active imagination, and he especially enjoyed reading Ernest Hemingway's and Jack London's stories about remote and isolated places. While at Janice's apartment, he started reading about Antarctica, and he quickly made up his mind to somehow get there himself. He figured the only way he'd ever do it was if he joined the Coast Guard. Sure enough, he enlisted and got himself assigned to an icebreaker, which went to Antarctica for six months. A picture shows Charlie standing on the deck of the ship with jagged ice floes behind him. He is tall, six foot four, handsome, with sparkling blue eyes and brown hair. His smile shows how happy he is, living his dreams of adventure.

In a letter to his parents, Charlie wrote:

> *I should have joined the Coast Guard years ago. It's unbelievable! Compared with the Marine Corps the Coast Guard is, well—there isn't any comparison actually. The guys are a lot friendlier and you can actually have a conversation with an officer. I'm aboard the* Staten Island. *The Navy built her after WWII, and we gave her to the Russians during the Eisenhower*

*Administration. And get this—the Russians got fed up
with her in the Arctic and just left her there. Well, the
Coast Guard went up there and claimed her. On the
engines, some of the pressure valves are in Russian!*

After serving on the West Coast and making the voyage to
Antarctica, Charlie was transferred to an East Coast station. At
this station, Charlie's independent streak landed him in serious
trouble. An officer who disliked Charlie found a reason to pun-
ish him and made him clean brass fittings on a cutter with a
toothbrush. When Charlie was finished, the officer called the
crew together, then stepped up to stand face-to-face with Charlie
and said, "Bucko, what do you have to say for yourself?" Charlie
answered that question by punching the officer in the nose.

Charlie was put in the brig—military jail—and later transferred to serve under Executive Petty Officer Brad Willey at
Point Allerton in Hull, Massachusetts. Willey later recalled, "You
can imagine the reputation he had. One morning reveille was
going, and Charlie didn't show up. I found him still asleep in his
bed. I took his mattress and flipped it, and he smacked into the
floor. He jumped up and glared at me, but then smiled and said,
'You've got a lot of guts.' Somehow that cemented a respect. He
was a bright guy, and could do just about anything he set his
mind to."

Pete Lafontaine, another officer at Point Allerton, says Charlie
was "a natural leader and rescuer." Lafontaine saw Charlie develop
from a brash and reckless youth to a mature, confident young

man: "He really found his niche when he became a coxswain. He never had to raise his voice to his crew, and they really responded to him. We had him out on so many rescues I lost count. He had a whole lot of heavy weather experience under his belt when the blizzard struck. Charlie would have gone a long way in the Coast Guard."

~

At Point Allerton Charlie trained several younger Coasties to be coxswains, one of whom was John Halter from Minnesota. Halter and Charlie became close friends, and Charlie confided that he wanted to be a writer and was working on a story set in Vietnam called "Guardian of the Rain," in which a young soldier's entire unit was ambushed while he sat alone in the rain on sentry duty. Halter thought Charlie looked a little like a young Ernest Hemingway: "He was a tall, powerful-looking man with dimples and laughing eyes."

After Halter completed his coxswain training, Charlie transferred up to Gloucester Station, but the two friends stayed in touch, with Halter making frequent visits to Gloucester. Charlie told Halter that Gloucester was the best station he'd ever served at.

Charlie had a zest for life as well. Another coxswain at Gloucester Station recalls that one afternoon he taught Charlie how to ride his motorcycle. "Well," says the coxswain, "the next day he shows up at the station in leather riding pants, biker's boots, and leather vest. He was hooked and ready to bike across America."

While at Gloucester, Charlie met his future fiancée, Sharon

Watts, and decided it was time to leave the Coast Guard and settle down.

Sharon wondered how he would adjust to civilian life. To her surprise, he did just fine, simply focusing his energies on his dozens of other interests. "He was beat coming home every night from his new job at the shipyard, but he truly liked his work and fellow coworkers. I loved watching him come through the door of our apartment with his ratty old jeans and flannel shirt." After dinner the couple would take quiet walks, often sneaking up to the Eastern Point Lighthouse to sit by the breakwater and watch the sunset over the harbor. At the breakwater, the couple would talk of their future together, which, of course, still involved the water.

Charlie had picked out a boat, and he talked about how someday Sharon and their kids would all enjoy it together. He also sketched out a design for his dream house, which he wanted to build overlooking the coast. He envisioned the family room to have nautical furnishings and feature his restored furniture, with a window looking out to sea.

When Charlie retired from the Coast Guard in 1977, his family was relieved, especially after he told them about the sea conditions he'd experienced during the rescue of the oil tanker *Chester Poling*. Sister Joan says, "Charlie had that marine mentality 'to leave no man behind,' and we knew he would do anything to help someone in need. So we were glad when he settled down with Sharon, and not on a Coast Guard patrol boat, figuring life would be a lot safer."

Charlie landed a job at the Marine Railway Company in Gloucester, where he met Doug Parsons. Doug recalls that all the workers had fun picking on the "new guy." One hot August day a flatbed truck pulled up to the shop with 450 bags of grit used in sandblasting, and each bag weighed one hundred pounds. There were no forklifts but rather a long line of workers to pass the bags down the line from the truck to inside the shop. They positioned Charlie right in the middle of the line and then went as fast as they could. "There was no way he could keep up," recalls Parsons, "and we were razzing him about that. It was like boot camp all over again. But Charlie knew how to handle it. He always had a big smile and was a riot to be around."

Parsons also remembers having serious discussions with Charlie, such as what they would do if caught in a desperate situation in bad seas. Charlie said he would tell his crew that if they ever got in real trouble, "Never leave the boat; the boat is your only chance."

Charlie had never been more happy and contented than in 1978. A lot had to do with Sharon. They met in January 1977, when Sharon was a teller at the Gloucester National Bank and Charlie was opening an account. Charlie asked Sharon out, and she said yes, attracted by Charlie's ear-to-ear smile. When Sharon brought Charlie home to have dinner with her family, she tried to play a little trick on him involving her twin sister. They had plans to go out after dinner, so Sharon went upstairs to change. Her twin sneaked upstairs as well and changed her clothes, then came back down and told Charlie she was ready to go, taking him by the arm and leading him outside. But Charlie immediately recognized the deception and said, "Where's Sharon?" Sharon's sister went back upstairs and proclaimed, "He's a keeper."

It didn't take long for Sharon and Charlie to fall in love, and they were engaged in less than a year. The wedding was planned for May 14, 1978. Charlie was still in the Coast Guard when the couple first met, and leaving was a difficult decision. But he told Sharon that after his experience with the *Chester Poling*, he should get out of the Coast Guard or he'd make her a widow.

"Charlie had only been in Gloucester a couple years," recalled Sharon, "but he really liked the town, and we dreamed of building our own home. In fact, the day before the blizzard, he sketched a floor plan of the house he wanted to have built. We were hoping it would be close to the ocean, because he loved the sea and said he always wanted to be near it. Even on vacations, we had to be by the sea. His favorite time was right after a big storm, when he could watch the surf. In that sense, he and Frank Quirk were two kindred spirits. They were the best of friends and really watched out for each other. Charlie had been out with Frank on the *Can Do* several times. When conditions were bad, Charlie would go to help out on piloting jobs. He was getting a good feel for what the *Can Do* could do in really bad seas."

Charlie used some of his free time to channel his energies into his latest writing project, a manuscript about a sea rescue that he hoped to have published as his first book. "It was remarkable how it mirrored the night of the blizzard," says Sharon. "He had the book about ninety percent complete, all handwritten in a spiral notebook. The book was about five men who set out during a winter storm to help some friends whose boat was in trouble."

Unfortunately, the manuscript titled *The Boat Job* was lost when Sharon's basement flooded several years after the blizzard. Charlie's sister Janice, however, had saved his preliminary book outline, and it does have some striking, eerie parallels to the night he went out on the *Can Do*. In sketching out the story, he wrote how "no one believes the weatherman who comes to the conclusion that this is the granddaddy of all northeasters. An intense low pressure system in the Ohio valley is moving northeast with a secondary low forming in Long Island Sound." When the systems converge, he wrote, "a huge storm is developing, hurricane winds, with twenty foot seas. Storm tide with moon tide in excess of fifteen feet [above normal]. Heavy snow/sleet."

Charlie's outline notes clearly show how he planned to combine some of his real-life experiences with his own rich imagination. Certain characters would be modeled after real people in the Coast Guard, events borrowed from the *Chester Poling* rescue, and incidents incorporated from his days at Point Allerton. He also had Frank and the *Can Do* in mind, noting that a pilot boat would join other Coast Guard boats going to the aid of the stricken tanker. His outline goes on to describe two lead characters who have marked similarities to Charlie and Frank, with a notation saying "the reader must feel the chemistry that makes these two men get along so well." Charlie then describes how

Salem Shipping Control picks up a Mayday call from a tanker in distress and how the actions of the two lead characters during the blizzard will determine whether they live or die.

And now, in the actual blizzard, Frank and Charlie were side by side in the pilothouse, drawing on every bit of their nautical know-how to keep the beleaguered *Can Do* afloat. In Charlie, Frank saw a younger but more gregarious version of himself, and he warmed to the big man's smile and self-deprecating humor. For Charlie, Frank was something of a role model, a veteran of the seas. Charlie was heartened by the fact that Frank could make his living on the ocean and still be involved in helping mariners in distress. And Charlie took note of Frank's family life, especially how the entire Quirk family made the *Can Do* their weekend home and how the boys could operate the boat as if they'd been at sea for years. It's no surprise that he told Sharon, "I want kids— not just a couple but a whole slew of them. Think of the times we'll have!"

DANGER ON THE
FORTY-FOUR

As the storm intensified, Mike Paradis had shifted his focus from a search-and-rescue mission for the *Global Hope* to a search for his own forty-four-foot patrol boat. He knew the boat was somewhere in the vicinity of Salem Sound. The potential for the patrol boat to lose power (as a result of their propellers hitting a rock and stalling the engine) and capsize was actually greater in ledge-strewn Salem Sound than it had been earlier on the open ocean.

Warren Andrews's concern for the Forty-Four was also growing by the minute. He was restless in his radio room, running his fingers through his wavy black hair, fidgeting in his seat with a helpless feeling. The idea came to him to have spotters looking for the Forty-Four along the shore. Andrews picked up the phone and began calling members of the Northeast Surf Patrol, asking them to take handheld marine radios and drive to various points along Salem Harbor's north side. Warren hoped that maybe one of these volunteers would spot the blue light on the Forty-Four and could then radio him with their position, so Andrews could guide the patrol boat into safe waters.

~

On board the Forty-Four, the crewmen were keeping their cool. Most of them had already experienced tough missions and dangerous seas. In fact, Bob Krom, the youngest of the group at nineteen, had been injured just a few months earlier on a rescue. Although he looked like he could be a defensive end in the NFL, the six-foot, seven-inch Krom found that he was no match for angry seas and pounding boats. He had been part of a crew on the Forty-Four that went out in a storm to rescue a man who was having a seizure on a slow-moving charter boat. When the Forty-Four reached the charter boat, they pulled up alongside and Krom went to help transfer the ill passenger onto the Coast Guard boat. Just as Krom grabbed the man, the two boats crashed together. Krom felt a searing pain in his right foot and looked down to see that the end of his boot had been sliced away, taking the tips of several toes in the process. Krom recalls that he and his crew first got the man with the seizure on board the Forty-Four, then Krom hobbled below. He wouldn't let the others take his boot off because he knew the injury was severe and he didn't want to see just how bad it was. He kept his foot elevated while the Forty-Four raced back to Gloucester. Krom ended up in the hospital, and although he lost part of four of his toes, his big toe was intact and his balance was not affected.

While the Blizzard of '78 was worse than anything the crew of the Forty-Four had ever seen, their training and prior missions helped keep them focused and working as a team while crowded together in the pilothouse. McIlvride was at the wheel; Desrosiers, the engineer, was to his left for quick access to the engine room if needed. Seamen Mathurin and Krom were to McIlvride's right. They took turns shining a flashlight on the compass, struggling with the malfunctioning radar, and peering out into the driving snow, hoping to see a buoy. As each wave broke over the stern, water rushed up in the cockpit, frequently reaching the thighs of the men. Being soaking wet in twenty-degree temperatures should have chilled the men to the bone, but they barely noticed the cold—too much was happening. Their muscles involuntarily coiled and tensed, ready to spring into action should the boat suddenly flounder. Adrenaline, at least in the short term, shut out the discomforts of being wet in a gale with windchill below zero. Surprisingly, none of the four were seasick.

Heading west-southwest, they were in extreme following seas—a situation that can cause pitchpoling, where the stern of the boat is lifted up and over the bow, causing the boat to flip. This can happen when, as each wave catches the boat, the stern tries to overtake the bow and the vessel begins to sideslip. Each time this happens, the propeller loses its effectiveness and the vessel is momentarily out of control.

"We were going at full speed," says McIlvride, "with each passing wave surging us forward at an accelerated pace, and usually knocking us off course. I had to fight to keep the boat from broaching [going sideways] on the face of the wave, and we'd get thrown off course as the wave passed. So, on the back of the wave, I'd look at the compass and get us back on course for a few seconds until the next wave came."

Mathurin recalls that they did see the light on Baker's Island and, as they entered Salem Sound, were probably somewhere near the tanker. He knew there was no way they were going to get any men off the tanker in thirty-foot seas, so their primary goal was to keep trying to grope their way to calmer waters. Without their fathometer, they were at a distinct disadvantage, because they had no idea of the depth of water they were in. And as each minute passed, spray continued to freeze on the Forty-Four, increasing its weight and reducing stability.

Mathurin and the others were expending incredible energy just to stay upright in the crowded pilothouse, because the boat was not only pitching up and down but also sliding from side to side.

"One of our pumps we were carrying to the tanker came loose below," says Krom. "I went down to secure it, but there was such unbelievable motion I was knocked to the deck. As I struggled with the pump, the big compartment heater was blowing directly on me. Between that and the boat's broaching and falling, I got sick and puked in the engine room. Even though it was freezing up above and we were constantly getting wet, anything was better than being down below. I went back up and continued to search for a buoy. We could barely hear each other shout because of howling wind and the snapping of the tattered plastic and canvas covering."

While the men on the Forty-Four did their best to avoid the ledges, the *Can Do* was on its way to look for them. As the pilot boat plowed out of Gloucester Harbor, Frank, Charlie, and the others prepared for the unknown.

"We're under way, Warren," radioed Frank. *"Just going up by the Coast Guard station here. Will see what it looks like outside. I don't know if we're going to get clobbered. If we can poke along that way, we might take a look around."*

Andrews responded, *"Roger, Frank. It is a beauty. We have very heavy snow, zero visibility, and the winds estimated here at sixty to seventy. I just hope my radio tower stands up."*

ROGUE WAVES AND DEAD ENGINES

While the Forty-Four struggled in Salem Sound, the *Can Do* cleared the breakwater of Gloucester Harbor. Although Paradis had already asked Frank what men were aboard the pilot boat, he did so again, stress edging into his voice: *"Frank, what do you have for crew?"*

In the heaving boat, Frank picked up the radio transmitter and snapped, *"Yeah, just stand by here."*

Although Frank didn't say any more for a few minutes, from the tone of his voice it was clear the boat required his full attention. The *Can Do* was now beyond the safety of Gloucester Harbor, and Frank, like McIlvride, was putting every ounce of energy and concentration into controlling the boat. Like a bucking horse that had been spooked, the *Can Do* seemed to have a mind of its own. Cresting seas hurled the pilot boat down enormous steep-faced waves so that the vessel literally surfed, going much faster than the skipper had intended. Frank worked the throttle and the rudder to control the pilot boat's power so that it rode the backs of the mountainous waves without actually going over. He worried his bow might bury in a trough.

A few minutes later, Paradis radioed the Forty-Four that the *Can Do* was heading down to assist them. "Although we never asked for help, we were relieved to hear the *Can Do* might be coming out," says Tom Desrosiers, "because we were still without radar and didn't know exactly where we were. Since Frank Quirk was a pilot boat captain, we knew that he had to know the area like the back of his hand. In the meantime, we tried to avoid the ledges and maybe find a buoy to tie up to."

Just minutes later, at eight thirty, the greatest fears of the Forty-Four crew were realized when they heard a bang as the boat struck an obstruction—likely some rocks. Both engines immediately stalled from the sudden hit.

This was the darkest moment for the crew of the Forty-Four. After running all the way from Gloucester, the men had taken comfort from the sound of the engines; when they conked out, the silence was eerie.

In the darkness, McIlvride, wet and weary, radioed Paradis that the engines were dead. The commanding officer shouted out, *"Drop your hook!"* and McIlvride answered, *"Roger."* Paradis was worried sick the boat would be hit broadside by a wave or maybe take a breaking wave over the stern. He knew these disasters could be avoided by setting anchor—the "hook"—because the anchor was attached to the bow, and when it took hold, the Forty-Four would swing around with its bow into the waves.

Although McIlvride had answered, "Roger," he had no intention of following that order. There was no way he was going to send one of the crew out on the bow to release the anchor and secure it. The boat was pitching like a roller coaster, and if the man fell off, he would die almost instantly. The skipper figured if the engines wouldn't restart, there might still be time to drop the anchor. The rest of the crew, of course, agreed with the decision, and they didn't waste a moment worrying about lying to Paradis. Their focus was on the engines.

~

Paradis's concern reached a new level, and it showed in his impatience. After waiting a few agonizing seconds, he came back on the radio: *"Have you restarted your engines?"*

"We're working on it."

"Let me know immediately."

When the engines died, Desrosiers, the engineer, flung open the hatch and ran below. He looked through the porthole into the engine room. He didn't see any water coming inside, so he went in. Everything looked in order, even the propeller shaft. Desrosiers figured he'd simply press the electric-start engine button and see what happened. The engines started, and that was the most beautiful sound the engineer had ever heard in his young life.

McIlvride quickly notified Paradis: *"Engines restarted at this time. We're going to try to circle into the wind and waves."*

"If you see any aid at all, make a real attempt to tie up to it or stay as near to it as possible. Commencing now, I want you men to give me a radio check every ten minutes."

"We are looking for an aid, but nothing in sight. We're still proceeding in slow."

Although the engines were working, the radar and depth finder were not, and should the Forty-Four slam into a ledge again, the engines might not restart. Paradis tried another suggestion for getting the radar back on track: *"Try tuning it down; there may be too much tune-up with the snow."*

"There's no result playing with the tuner. We tried, but there's just no picture at all."

The worrying went on for Paradis, and he contacted Frank to give him an update and to let him know his help was still needed: *"Frank, whatever he hit, he's clear of it. He's maneuvering. Totally disoriented at this time. He doesn't have compass or radar. If it's at all possible, I'd appreciate it if you would head over that way."*

~

Additional assistance was on the way as the 95-foot cutter *Cape George* slowly headed north from Boston and the 210-foot cutter *Decisive* was dispatched from its anchorage just off Provincetown,

Massachusetts. However, both ships had their own troubles, and they were heading into the seas and wind, which made for a snail-like pace. Bob Donovan was a twenty-year-old seaman at the wheel of the *Cape George*, working alongside Myron Verville and Skipper Glen Snyder. Now that the *Cape George* was outside Boston Harbor, Donovan knew there was no turning back, and he gripped the wheel hard. The wheel was four feet in diameter and power assisted, but it was still difficult to control. But the worst part for Donovan was that he couldn't see the towering waves; he could only feel them. The cutter lifted almost straight up, then slammed back down.

Donovan used the wheel as much for support to keep on his feet as for steerage. His arms had quickly become black-and-blue from banging into the edge of the wheel. He felt like he was in the air more than on the deck as the cutter pitched violently on its northward journey. Around him, crewmates would be standing one minute, then hurled to the deck the next. Wind gusts had now hit one hundred miles per hour, and some of the waves were thirty feet.

~

While Donovan manned the wheel, Verville read the charts and gave advice to Skipper Snyder, who then checked the compass course and the loran-C before making the final decisions on their course and speed. While they were physically taking a pounding, Donovan thought that Tom Murrin, one of the engineers, had the toughest assignment of all. Donovan later recalled that

Murrin "was in the engine control booth, alone, for the entire trip. It was no bigger than a telephone booth and extremely hot. I don't know how he managed. When he got out, he was a little wild from going through that experience. It was like being locked in a cage and placed inside a clothes dryer—and expected to do your job. I'm now a commercial fisherman, and have been for some time, and I've never seen conditions like that night—not even close."

Vern DePietro, also on the *Cape George*, had only been in the Coast Guard for six months, and he took his cues from the more seasoned men. Despite the cold temperatures on the bridge, he was sweating beneath his coat. "Even though I was the new guy," says DePietro, "I knew we were in serious trouble just by the way some of the more experienced guys were acting. They were deadly serious, saying very little, and you could see the stress in their eyes. There were about twelve guys on board, and I was one of the men up on the bridge acting as a lookout, but of course I couldn't see anything. Our radar wasn't worth a damn because there was so much clutter from snow. Half the time I was puking my guts out. One way to alleviate seasickness is to get fresh air and watch the seas and the horizon, but that night it would be suicide to go outside. The only time we could see the ocean was when it was literally on top of us. One thing I do remember was hearing Frank Quirk on the radio having a discussion with Gloucester and then making the decision to go out."

Conditions were a little better on the larger cutter, the *Decisive*, but not much. Damage Controlman Jim Quinn was part of the engineering group aboard the 210-foot cutter, and he remembers that the *Decisive* encountered difficulties from the very start. The anchor could not be lifted onto the vessel because it was fouled in a cable. Quinn strapped a harness on, grabbed a cutting torch, and then leaned over the side of the ship to try to free the anchor. The seas were building, and Quinn had to time each swell perfectly as he bent over the rail and began cutting. It took a while, but eventually he freed the anchor. The *Decisive* then got under way, but because the cutter was going into the seas, Quinn estimates it was only able to make five nautical miles per hour as the seas pounded the bow.

Although the *Decisive* dwarfed the *Can Do* and the forty-four-footer, the men on board the cutter still didn't feel safe, because of the extreme seas. "If one thing went wrong, we knew we could be in serious trouble," says Quinn. "It was a fine line between making it and not making it. One of my worries was that we were taking green seas [not just the tops of waves] over the stern and our exhaust vents were horizontal, so water could have gone into the engines. If we lost power, I'm sure we would have capsized. I remember looking out the mess deck windows that are normally about eight feet above the water, and it was like looking into an aquarium. One rogue wave hit us, and it sent everything and everybody over and down on the deck."

A rogue wave is one that is not in step with the other waves and is usually much larger, often catching the crew by surprise. It can come out of calm seas or heavy seas but always poses a danger because of its unexpected nature. In 1995 during rough seas, the *Queen Elizabeth II*, a 963-foot-long cruise ship with a weight of 70,327 gross tons, took a rogue wave directly over the bow while crossing the North Atlantic. The crewmen in the wheelhouse said they saw the wave approach out of the darkness and it felt as if time slowed as they watched it advance, astonished that the crest of the wave was level with their line of vision on the bridge, which was ninety-five feet above the sea surface. The sea cascaded over the forward deck and the bridge, temporarily blinding the men in the wheelhouse, bending steel railings, and denting deck plating. The wave was so powerful it even caved in the Grand Lounge windows, located aft of (behind) the wheelhouse. Canadian weather buoys later confirmed the rogue wave's massive size, measuring it at exactly ninety-eight feet.

Mariners who have encountered rogue waves sometimes call them holes in the seas because of the deep trough that precedes the steep forward face of the wave. The reason that a single wave is larger than all others is not entirely clear. Some experts theorize that rogue waves form when three or more smaller waves coalesce into an unusually large one. Or rogue waves might originate when currents or random eddies meet steady wind-produced incoming wave swells head-on. The interaction reduces the spacing between waves, creating a single giant wave and often even changing its direction. Off the eastern coast of the U.S., the northeast-flowing Gulf Stream may account for monster waves when it interrupts storm-produced waves moving in the opposite direction. Originating in the warm waters in the eastern part of the Gulf of Mexico, the Gulf Stream is about fifty miles wide and three thousand feet deep.

Topography of the ocean's floor may also play a role in the formation of rogue waves, particularly when swells from a distant storm move over an area of reduced water depth. Another possible cause for rogue wave creation is several different wave trains of differing speeds and directions meeting at the same time, briefly forming an extreme wave. Scientists are also analyzing the release of natural gas from the ocean's floor and its effects on waves.

One thing for certain is that on a storm-ravaged sea like the night of February 6, 1978, the waves were not uniform. Waves of twenty-five to thirty-five feet prowled the sea, using the cover of darkness to surprise anyone who dared to be out. There was no time for humans to react, but instead they must trust in the seaworthiness of boats that were already at their limits.

The *Decisive* recovered from the rogue wave and continued on its north-northwest course. However, the waves were continuing to grow as the storm exploded in intensity during the early evening hours. With each passing minute, the waves had a chance to grow larger because of the three components that determine wave size: the speed of the wind, the amount of time the wind blows, and the fetch, the distance of open water over which the wind is blowing. Just as troubling, visibility dropped from half a mile to zero during that same time period.

The *Can Do* was out on the open ocean just as the seas were beginning to show their full fury. In the pilothouse Charlie was standing next to Frank at the wheel. Each time the boat rode up and out of a trough, they anxiously glanced at the radar screen for the brief view of what was ahead. As the *Can Do* crested the next wave and was propelled downward, green water temporarily engulfed the boat, making the men feel entombed. While fear might grip other experienced mariners in this situation, Charlie and Frank kept their cool. Together, they had been through an eerily similar rescue effort just a year before.

THE RESCUE OF THE
CHESTER POLING

The rescue Frank and Charlie had participated in happened a year earlier, on January 10, 1977. Both men, piloting separate boats, had responded to the Mayday of a 282-foot coastal tanker, the *Chester Poling*. The similarities between the *Poling* rescue and the Blizzard of 1978 are striking: both involved tankers in jeopardy, the same group of boats (the *Can Do, Cape George*, and *Cape Cross*, and the forty-one- and forty-four-footers) went to the rescue, and some of the same people responded.

On the morning of the *Chester Poling*'s fateful voyage, the tanker was in port in Everett, Massachusetts, having just off-loaded a cargo of kerosene. Captain Charles Burgess heard a weather forecast calling for winds of ten to twenty knots, increasing to twenty-five to thirty-five. Burgess was an experienced captain in his fifties, and he felt his ship could handle the bad weather, so he began the next phase of his voyage, heading north toward New Hampshire.

Only an hour into the trip, the vessel was pounded by waves larger than the ten-footers the weather service had forecast for the morning. By nine A.M. seas had reached twenty feet, with approximately one hundred fifty feet between crests. An hour later, while standing in the wheelhouse, Burgess was startled by a loud banging sound; he concluded something had come adrift and was striking the hull. Crewman Harry Selleck was with the captain and carefully inched his way out on the deck in the cold, slicing rain but could see nothing amiss.

Thirty-five minutes later, Selleck looked out a forward porthole and saw "a sea of enormous proportions . . . pick up the ship." Selleck later described what happened next: "The bow came down and buried into a wall of sea that was twice the size of the normal seas that had been reported. The ship vibrated. She shook as she was coming down as if someone was pulling her back and forth, like seesawing."

Another wave hit the ship, followed by a sickening crunching sound and a grinding reverberation of twisted metal. Selleck and Burgess looked aft of the wheelhouse and could not believe their eyes—the ship had broken in two.

The bow and the stern section tilted toward where the break occurred, but each stayed afloat. With an alarm sounding, the five men on the aft section ran from below up to the sloping deck and stared in horror: A segment of deck plating was the only thing connecting the two sections, preventing them from drifting apart. Crew members rushed to get life jackets on, fearing the sections of the *Chester Poling* would sink within seconds.

In a stroke of good fortune, the VHF-FM radio in the pilot-house still worked because it was battery powered. Captain Burgess immediately called out a Mayday message on channel 13, followed by a desperate plea: *"We are six miles off Cape Ann! Don't know how much longer we can stay afloat!"*

"Be advised the cutter Cape George *is on the way,"* replied Coast Guard Group Boston.

"We split in two," shouted Burgess, *"and don't know how long we can stay afloat. Not sinking yet, but we might be any minute."*

"Are there any persons on board the other section?"

"We have five members aft!"

"Can you see the aft section?"

"No, too much seas coming over!"

The nearest Coast Guard station was Gloucester, where the cutters *Cape George* and *Cape Cross* were temporarily berthed at their heavy weather mooring at the State Pier. Upon receiving the Mayday, Gloucester Coast Guard asked all nearby vessels to proceed to the scene and dispatched both ninety-five-foot cutters, as well as its forty-one- and forty-four-foot patrol boats to the rescue.

Frank heard the Mayday as well and radioed the Coast Guard that he was heading to the *Poling* to assist in whatever way he could. Quirk was accompanied by Bill Lee, who later said, "This was something you just do when other fishermen or mariners are in danger of drowning; it's like firemen responding to an alarm. I trusted Frank, and knew he'd make the right decisions."

The *Cape George* was able to get under way within ten minutes of receiving the call, but the *Cape Cross* had just come off patrol and was undergoing maintenance, delaying its departure for forty-five minutes.

Aboard the *Cape Cross* was eighteen-year-old Larry Zaker, just three weeks out of boot camp. On that January day, he received a harrowing initiation into his new profession. "We got under way in a little more than an hour, and as soon as we passed the breakwater, we were slammed. The seas were so bad I said to myself, 'This is the day I'm gonna die.' It was so rough I remember the refrigerator was ripped right off the bulkhead."

~

The *Can Do* was slowed by the huge seas but continued east to the *Chester Poling*. Frank was in communication with all the boats as well as with the onshore Coast Guard coordinators. He radioed the Coast Guard, telling them, *"We are taking a real beating, but making progress."*

Frank was also able to raise Captain Burgess on the radio, offering encouragement, knowing that Burgess faced death at any moment.

"Can Do to Chester Poling."

"This is Poling."

"The ninety-five [Cape George] is up ahead, and we are going by the number two buoy. The Forty-Four is also up ahead. Help is on the way; hang in there."

"When you come," said Burgess, *"get the crew off first, and I'll stand by. We might have to get a towline. . . ."*

Ever pragmatic, Frank responded, *"Well, let's just worry about people first, and then we'll see about that."*

While Frank was making progress, the forty-one-footer was being tossed about like flotsam. Skippered by coxswain John Burlingham, the boat had lost most of its electronics, and the shrieking wind made it difficult to be heard on the radio. Burlingham could not head back to port because he was afraid the boat would capsize if a wave caught them broadside before the turn was completed. Burlingham's only option was to motor all the way to the tanker and then try to make the turn on *Poling's* lee (downwind and sheltered) side, where he hoped the waves might be a bit smaller.

Commanding Officer Paradis at Station Gloucester understood their predicament, and he radioed the *Cape George*, *"Be advised that the Forty-One-footer is just holding its own and is trying to turn around and come back in. The Forty-Four is still out there and trying to find you."*

Frank was monitoring these communications and was on the lookout for both the Forty-One and Forty-Four, knowing they were vulnerable. Frank felt a little vulnerable himself and radioed the *Cape Cross*, *"Don't run me over on the way out; you might not see me with seas so big."*

When Boston heard this, they asked the *Can Do* for an update on weather conditions. Frank responded, *"Twenty to twenty-five seas. It's really howling; we are two miles east of the number two buoy."*

While the *Cape Cross*, the *Can Do*, and the other boats were making their way to the scene, the *Cape George* arrived at the stricken tanker in just under an hour. James Loew, commanding officer of the *Cape George*, attempted to maneuver his cutter alongside the bow section of the tanker. He quickly abandoned the effort, however, realizing the seas were so violent that his own boat might be crushed or swamped by the stern of the *Poling*.

Loew radioed Captain Burgess, *"Your bow is really swinging around. Is there any way that your crew could get into a life raft and get away from the boat? Then we could pick them up?"*

Burgess replied this could not be done.

Loew considered floating a raft toward the tanker, but the two sections of the *Chester Poling* were finally pulling apart the narrow deck plating that connected them. The bow and stern suddenly separated, then pounded upon each other, with the bow listing heavily as seas poured into the wheelhouse portholes.

The forty-four-foot patrol boat arrived on the scene with Charlie Bucko as the coxswain. He radioed to the other boats that his radar had been knocked out but he could see the tanker. The *Cape George* asked if the Forty-Four, given its smaller size, could get alongside the tanker. But the Forty-Four had the same problem as the cutter: the tanker sections were rising and falling in heavy seas, making it impossible to get closer. Charlie maneuvered his boat as close as he dared and held position, ready to act if any of the tanker's crewmen leaped into the sea.

Soon Frank on the *Can Do* and Burlingham on the Forty-One arrived on the scene. Burlingham recalls that his mission was complicated when a particularly large wave hit the boat, causing a crewman to do a free fall, injuring his back and neck. Burlingham couldn't turn around because he needed to get out into deeper water.

Burlingham and his crew made a decision and announced it on the radio: *"I'm going to attempt to get back. I've got a man down with a pretty good back injury—he says his legs are going numb."*

Gloucester asked, *"Who is the injured man?"*

"It's the new seaman, Cavanaugh. He has not moved, but he's conscious."

Bill Cavanaugh remembers that fall as if it happened yesterday: "I was down below preparing a Stokes Litter [a wire basket to scoop survivors out of the ocean] when we climbed up a huge sea. Then the boat fell off the crest like an elevator would drop if it lost its cables. I was literally weightless, being pushed up against the ceiling for a couple seconds; then when the boat smashed down, I slammed into the deck. I remember looking at this pair of legs beneath my body wondering whose they were because I couldn't feel anything. I later found out I had broken my neck. On the ride back in, I thought I was paralyzed for life. In fact, it took several days of being in traction before there was any movement or sensation in my legs. When the nerves first started responding, the pain was almost unbearable, and that went on for almost two weeks."

Frank heard the communications from the Forty-One. Knowing they had an injured man on board and were without navigational electronics, Frank radioed the Forty-One and told them he would be looking for them to guide the boat back to Gloucester, adding, *"I've never seen seas like this."* He escorted the boat back and then turned right around, steaming back to the tanker, making better time because the wind had blown the tanker sections toward land.

Meanwhile Captain Burgess knew the bow wouldn't stay afloat much longer. He radioed the *Cape George*: *"As soon as she starts to go down, we are going to jump. She's breaking up now more than ever."*

Loew shouted for the captain to hang on a little longer, because his crew was going to try to float a life raft to Burgess and Selleck and then haul them back. Again, however, conditions prevented success. Loew was relaying this latest setback to Gloucester when he suddenly barked, *"Both men are in the water! Don't have time to talk."*

Five minutes later, Loew shouted, *"I just picked up one man in the water and have another man in the water! Stand by."*

The man the *Cape George* picked up was Captain Burgess, but they were unable to get Selleck on the first pass. The freezing water all but paralyzed Selleck. He later told the Coast Guard,

"The only thing that kept me alive was that I knew the cutter *Cape George* knew they had missed me and that I was still out there. There were times when I was going to give up. I was going to take off my life jacket and forget it, but they came back and threw heaving lines. I couldn't grab the heaving lines because my hands were pretty well frozen and I didn't have the strength. I got hold of the net they had over the side. I grabbed it the first time and let go, and then I grabbed it the second time . . . They dragged me aboard."

Charlie Bucko, on the Forty-Four, stayed on the scene to assist the *Cape George* if needed. But his boat had suffered the same fate as the Forty-One, losing its navigational equipment. Moreover, the seas had taken a toll on his crew. Engineer Charlie Krocker had been knocked unconscious while making an adjustment in the engine room, and needed medical attention fast. Bucko also was very aware that he was putting his entire crew at risk if he kept the boat out without an engineer in extreme seas. Should the engines die and not be immediately restarted, the Forty-Four would capsize.

When he heard that the much larger *Cape Cross* would arrive within a couple of minutes, he made a decision to return to port and get the injured man medical attention. First, however, he needed to turn the vessel. He motored in close to the lee side of the *Poling*'s stern, carefully watching the waves while judging the distance separating the waves. He made his move between waves, working the wheel and the throttle, turning the boat as quickly as possible, then dashing back toward Gloucester and a waiting ambulance.

While Burgess and Selleck were being rescued, the wind was blowing the stern section toward the rocky shore of Gloucester's Eastern Point. Jim Loew expressed his concern: *"We are blowing really fast toward Eastern Point; the tanker may hit the breakwater soon."*

Luckily, a Coast Guard helicopter from Coast Guard Air Station Cape Cod and the *Cape Cross* arrived on the scene just a minute later to try to save the men on the stern. The *Cape Cross* maneuvered closer, and the helicopter, piloted by Lieutenant James B. (Brian) Wallace, hovered above the stern, struggling to maintain position in the sixty-knot winds. Wallace kept the helicopter approximately eighty feet above the water and only twenty feet above the stern of the *Poling*. "We wanted," says Wallace, "to be as close as possible so I'd have some kind of visual reference with the tanker. The conditions were absolutely awful. I even radioed my base that if they didn't hear from us for a while, that meant we had crashed."

The helicopter hoist operator, Petty Officer Reginald Lavoie, lowered a steel rescue basket with a guideline attached. Joao Gilmete, the *Chester Poling's* cook, was the first to enter the basket. The basket—with the cook hanging on inside—was pushed by the wind into the deck awning pipe framework and then spilled over the side of the ship and into the sea. Fortunately, the cook held on and Lavoie was able to raise the basket from the water, bringing the man into the helicopter unharmed.

The basket was lowered again, and this time it was Able Seaman Joao daRosa's turn to be rescued. Earlier he had changed out of his wet clothing, but in his haste, he forgot to put his life jacket back on. By this time, the seas had pushed the stern to within two thousand yards of Eastern Point, where the surf smashing against the rocks made a thunderous and nerve-racking clamor. Instead of waiting for the basket to reach an open part of the deck, daRosa climbed atop some oil drums and tried to step into the basket as it hovered outside of the ship's railing. As daRosa reached for the basket and raised one leg, the basket swung away, and he fell.

He tumbled into the ocean, surfaced once, then sank again. He reappeared a second time, only now facedown, floating with arms spread-eagle, drifting away from the stern. Pilot Wallace immediately banked the helicopter lower toward the floating seaman and Lavoie positioned the basket downwind of daRosa, just below the water's surface. The pilot inched the helo closer to the victim, and Lavoie attempted to scoop daRosa up by trailing the rescue basket beneath him. The waves kept the unconscious sailor in motion, rising and falling, and the basket could not be aligned for the scoop. Wallace was faced with a difficult decision: keep trying to scoop daRosa or return to the stern of the *Poling* before it went down with the remaining men on board. Looking below at daRosa, floating facedown, Wallace knew the man was dead, and he turned the helicopter back toward the living.

Frank heard that daRosa's body was drifting from the scene and radioed, *"We are at the breakwater, and we'll try and pick up that last man as soon as possible!"*

Three men were now left on board the stern, knowing that both jumping overboard toward the *Cape Cross* and trying to enter the rescue basket were fraught with risk. The trio made their decision and jumped overboard.

Two of them were soon rescued by the crew of the *Cape Cross*. The third man still in the water was Chief Mate Charles Lord, a nonswimmer. He had floated away from the other two men and was about to be lost in the swirling seas when helicopter pilot Wallace spotted him. Lord wasn't moving, but he was floating faceup on his back. The chopper pilot ordered the rescue basket lowered again, and he flew slowly over Lord, towing the basket behind in the water. "We lowered all two hundred feet of cable," says Wallace. "I remember one of the crew said there was a good chance that the cable might get wrapped around the victim's neck, and I shouted back, 'That's the chance we take; if we don't get him right away, he's dead from the cold.'"

On the third pass, the basket aligned perfectly with the immobile Lord, and he was scooped in and upward to safety. "Of all the people I've rescued over the years," says Wallace, "that guy was the closest to death of them all. I wonder if he knows how lucky he was. Getting him in the basket in those kinds of seas was like threading a needle in a hurricane—we all got lucky."

The helicopter and the *Cape Cross* left the scene, but Quirk and his crew continued looking for the body of daRosa. Frank gave a final update: *"Seas are twenty to twenty-five with some up to thirty. Seeing some debris but not spotting the stern section. [It had sunk.] We'll keep looking, but the radar is not doing too good because half the time the antenna is almost in the water. It's a miracle anyone got off alive; you wouldn't believe it out here."*

~

Frank Quirk hated to leave anyone at sea, even the dead, thinking of the effect on the family. In his career as a pilot boat operator, he often searched for missing sailors, without pay, just because it was the right thing to do. Warren Andrews later said, "That was Frank, always thinking about others. I recall when a diver drowned off Magnolia, Frank spent forty-eight straight hours looking for the man—a man he never even knew."

For their actions in aiding the mariners aboard the *Chester Poling*, Frank, Charlie Bucko, Jim Loew, and the other skippers involved received Gloucester's prestigious Mariner's Medal. Frank also received the Coast Guard's Public Service Commendation.

Jim Loew, the *Cape George* skipper, expressed the sentiments of all the Coast Guard personnel involved that day: "Just to know Frank was heading out to the *Poling* was real comforting because any one of us could have gotten into trouble and needed help. The *Can Do* was aptly named."

Later, in a formal service at the Coast Guard Station Gloucester, Frank was honored personally by the admiral. The press was there, and a picture was taken that, in retrospect, is rather chilling. In the photo, Frank Quirk and Charlie Bucko are shaking hands in the warm spring sunshine, discussing that terrible storm that split the *Chester Poling* in two.

A year later, the Blizzard of '78 drew these two men together for a rescue that was just as ferocious and twice as dangerous.

A STORM LIKE NO OTHER

The intensity of the Blizzard of 1978 surpassed that of any other winter storm experienced in southern New England in the last one hundred years. This monster was not just a blizzard but really a winter hurricane, with winds officially clocked at ninety-two miles per hour and unofficial recordings exceeding one hundred miles per hour. (Meteorologists refer to this storm as an "extratropical hurricane," which has a cold core distinguishing it from the usual autumn hurricane.) Satellite photos taken throughout Monday, February 6, show the cloud mass of the storm becoming more and more organized, taking on the well-defined look of a hurricane as the storm intensified and moved up the Eastern Seaboard, parallel to the coasts of New Jersey; Long Island, New York; and Rhode Island.

The storm developed when an upper-level low-pressure system moved southeastward out of Canada and intercepted a sea-level low-pressure system off the mid–Atlantic coast. The result was an explosively intensifying counterclockwise circulation that drew in surrounding air currents and blew them straight up and out of the organizing mass. A sleeping lion had begun to stir.

The storm headed north along the coast, strengthening rapidly as it picked up moisture and heat energy from the Gulf Stream–fed ocean while pulling in arctic air from the northwest. As the storm approached Long Island late that Monday night, it stalled due to a blocking ridge of cold, heavy polar air to the north. This caused the storm to gather all its strength and hurl it at the Bay State's coast for hours upon hours, time for the wind to generate great waves and drive the ocean ashore. In fact, as is common with such nor'easters, the strongest winds were some distance north of the storm's center, placing them off the Gloucester coastline. Analysis of weather charts showed isobars radiating out from the storm's center in all directions but packed closest together to the north of the storm. Each isobar represents a line of pressure, and lines close together depict great pressure changes over a short distance, or what meteorologists refer to as a tight pressure gradient. The clashing of pressure systems causes the most severe wind. The isobars on a weather map are reminiscent of the contours on a topographical map. Just as the elevation lines of a topographical map clustered together indicate the steepest hills, the presence of isobars close together on a weather map depicts the greatest pressure gradients. And just as water flows faster down that steep slope depicted on a topographical map, the air flows that much faster where the pressure gradient is tight on the weather map. On that fateful night in February 1978, Gloucester lay under the steepest part of that atmospheric slope. The resulting winds churned the sea into mountains of water.

Snowstorms can pelt New England anytime from November through April, but February has often been the month for the most severe snowstorms, in the form of nor'easters. Commonly, December and January have a jet stream that runs directly across the country, but in February variations to the jet stream occur more frequently, causing arctic air to plunge southward and collide with low-pressure systems and the fuel of subtropical air off the southeast United States coast. The offspring is a coastal nor'easter with the potential to intensify explosively, a process meteorologists term bombogenesis.

Adding to the potential for a significant snowfall along coastal New England is the fact that ocean temperatures usually reach their coldest during February. Had the *Chester Poling* sunk in February rather than January, it's likely there would have been more than one casualty. The storm that broke the tanker in two was vicious enough, but rain rather than snow was falling, keeping the temperature just high enough to prevent icing on the decks of the *Cape George* and *Cape Cross*. Although the helicopter crew that rescued several of the seamen risked their lives going out in such conditions, they never would have considered flying had it been snowing during that gale.

Along the coast the storm exploded just as the Forty-Four and the *Can Do* set out to sea. This was about the time when coastal communities began experiencing the havoc created by a surging ocean advancing far beyond its usual shoreline levels. In Rockport, cars were flung into the Old Harbor, along with a house. Bearskin Neck houses were crushed, then ripped by the seas, including the red wooden building known as Motif #1, a popular subject for artists. Car-size granite blocks protecting nearby Pigeon Cove, which had stood for a century, were knocked over as if made of Styrofoam. A few miles south, Marblehead Neck was cut off from the rest of the town as boulders the size of armchairs were hurled onto the causeway. In Nahant a man drowned when seas flooded his basement apartment. On Boston's south shore, in communities such as Scituate, Hull, and Marshfield, boats were ripped from their moorings and dumped on streets, in front yards, and sometimes right on top of houses. The scene was chaotic, with cars, boats, furniture, and appliances all mixed together, bobbing in the rising water that surrounded entire neighborhoods.

Up and down the Massachusetts coast, seawalls were flattened and hundreds of residents became trapped in their houses, encircled by swirling water that prevented them from running to higher ground. Police and fire departments were inundated with calls but often could not reach the danger areas because of flooded and snow-clogged roadways. The National Guard was called in to bring heavy equipment, such as front-end loaders and amphibious vehicles, to the affected towns, but it took several hours for them to arrive. In the meantime, trapped residents waited out the night with neither heat nor power.

~

One resident described how the evening conditions steadily worsened and with each passing hour her fear increased: "At first the house was shaken by the howling wind; then it was the spray off the ocean. Later the ocean itself was banging on the house. But what really shook me was when the sea started flinging fist-size cobbles into the walls, making sounds like gunshots. We knew our home's walls were starting to give way, but we just had to wait until help arrived—there was nowhere we could go."

Particularly hard hit was Revere, just north of Boston and south of Salem. Fires broke out in several houses due to electrical problems and flooded cellars, but firefighters could not reach the homes because the streets were impassible. Three homes were totally leveled, and several others suffered extensive damage from fire. However, it was the breaching of the seawall that did the most damage, and that occurred at eight thirty P.M., about the same time McIlvride and crew lost their engines.

"I thought I was going to die," reported Revere resident Anthony Chiarella to *Time* magazine, describing how he retreated to his attic with his dog, wondering when the house would be swept away. Other families slept in shifts so they wouldn't be caught unawares if the walls gave way. One elderly woman sat up on her kitchen sink as the water rose around her. All the doors were blocked by chunks of ice, so she started to go out the window to try to swim for higher ground. Luckily a neighbor saw her and told her to hang on. He then put on his scuba gear, swam over, and helped her swim with him to his house.

The ordeal had a lasting impact, what we would now refer to as post-traumatic stress disorder. A woman at a shelter was interviewed on TV and asked if she was anxious to get home. "I'm scared to go home," she said. "I don't want to go home. I don't want any part of that house. I'm terrified." In Revere alone, two thousand helpless and homeless people were sheltered at the high school.

The storm surge that pounded Revere and other coastal communities was being assisted by a new moon tide, often called a spring tide, which creates tides higher than normal. On the night of February 6, the moon was also in perigee (closest to the earth), which means the sun, earth, and moon were aligned in such a way that both the sun and the moon were pulling on the oceans. The largest astronomical tides occur when both spring tides and perigee tides coincide, which was exactly what happened during the blizzard. Couple that phenomenon with the onshore hurricane-force winds produced by the blizzard, and you have a recipe for disaster. In essence, the moon, sun, and wind were all working in perfect sync to produce the most damage possible. If one was so inclined as to look beyond coincidence, it was almost as if the storm had celestial help, in a sinister plot to do harm.

Inland the problem was snow. Snow falling harder than anyone had ever seen. Commuters were lulled into thinking they could make it home without too much trouble, because they had just been through a record-breaking snowfall three weeks earlier with no major traffic headaches. But on February 6, people were caught off guard. Weather forecasts had called for snow to start in the early morning hours, and when commuters awoke to snow-free skies, some figured the storm had gone out to sea or would be relatively benign. Employers thought the same thing, and even though it started snowing in the Boston area around eleven A.M., most employers were reluctant to release their employees. The lucky workers—or perhaps the smart ones—didn't wait for permission to leave when they saw how hard it was snowing by noon. Those who left before two P.M. generally made it home, while those who waited for an official office closing (which in most businesses came between two and three P.M.) found themselves in gridlocked traffic. Rush hour came early, but traffic wasn't moving, because the snow had caused enough spinouts to clog the highways.

Two of the worst areas were Route 128, the main artery that loops to the west and north around Boston, and Interstate 95, connecting Massachusetts and Rhode Island. Thousands of people were stuck in their cars, waiting helplessly as snowdrifts entombed them. Many were rescued Monday evening by police, National Guard, or private citizens on snowmobiles, but scores of others spent a harrowing night trapped in their cars. Some died of exposure when they ran out of gas trying to keep the car warm or while walking for help, and others succumbed to carbon monoxide poisoning caused by buildups of the deadly fumes in the cars.

The governors of Massachusetts and Rhode Island found that even with the aid of the National Guard, their emergency personnel were overwhelmed, and federal troops and equipment were called in. Every effort was made to keep one runway open at Boston's Logan Airport and another at Providence's Green Airport to allow the giant army cargo planes to land. Snowplow operators worked around the clock to keep sixty-foot-wide strips snow-free the length of the runways, but these efforts were hampered by the wind—eight-foot drifts were piling up as fast as workers could push the snow aside. When the federal troops did arrive, they were able to relieve some of the National Guard and local police who were needed to establish order in Boston and Providence where looting was occurring.

The American Red Cross reported ninety-nine deaths and more than thirty-nine thousand people stranded or forced from their homes by the storm. More than seventeen hundred homes were destroyed or damaged. Most of the deaths and destruction occurred in Massachusetts and Rhode Island, which took the full brunt of the storm. However, Maine, New Hampshire, Connecticut, and New York were hard hit, especially eastern areas, and as in Massachusetts, the coastal areas saw the seas turn furious in just a short period of time.

Just before the Forty-Four hit the underwater obstruction, Warren Andrews had made a series of telephone calls to members of the Northeast Surf Patrol. He explained the Forty-Four was lost somewhere in Salem Sound, and he asked Surf Patrol members to take up positions along the coast of Beverly, on the northwest side of Salem Sound. He wanted them to keep a lookout for the lights on the Forty-Four and, if they should see anything, radio back immediately. Warren would then radio the Forty-Four crew and be able to tell them exactly where they were and, with the aid of the Surf Patrol spotters, help guide them into Beverly Harbor.

Around nine P.M., a Surf Patrol shore spotter thought he saw the lights of the Forty-Four and excitedly called Warren: *"Unit one-seventy-two with possible sighting! I'm at Hospital Point Light and looking due east, and I just caught three flashes of a light. It might be the Coast Guard boat. If it is, it's in close to shore. It's a white to white-green light, kind of a high-intensity type light."*

A few minutes later, the spotter called again: *"Warren, I just saw a flash, and if he's heading in, he's close enough."*

The spotter was concerned because the shoreline is a jumble of jagged rocks, and with fifteen-foot seas within the sound, the Forty-Four would be crushed on the rocks if it got too close. Using his handheld FM radio, the spotter was able to talk directly with McIlvride and warn him away from the shore. The Forty-Four crew now kept an extra-sharp lookout and made sure they didn't veer any closer to the north, where the spiked granite shoreline lies. They still believed they could grope their way to safety, avoid having to drop anchor, and attempt to ride out the storm. McIlvride also knew that if worse came to worst—if the engines quit and the anchor wouldn't bite—they might be able to survive by going below and letting the boat crash into shore. "One of the men who trained me," says McIlvride, "used to say if your worst nightmare comes true and the Forty-Four is heading into rocks or the shore, go down below and batten all hatches. He thought that since the boat was built like a tank, we might be bloody and bruised, but we'd have a shot at surviving."

The one weakness in this approach was that the crew had to have time to get below and secure the main hatch. And since they would only resort to this tactic as a last-ditch effort to save themselves, the four men were going to stay up on the bridge as long as the engines were running. In the dark, however, they could be fifty feet from shore and not know it until it was too late, when there was no time to scramble below. They could not see the shoreline or hear the crashing surf on rocks because of the shrieking wind.

The crew of McIlvride, Krom, Desrosiers, and Mathurin figured they had made it this far and, with a little luck, would find their way to safe harbor. In fact, they staked their lives on their ability to maneuver their boat in ledge-infested waters rather than leaving their fate in the hands of the anchor or locking themselves below.

SWEPT OVER WITH A CRASH

The news that the Forty-Four had been sighted was certainly good, showing that progress was being made. The spotter, however, reported they were just two hundred yards off the rocky ledge of Hospital Point, and Paradis immediately considered the shallow water. He stood up in the communications room, running his fingers through his white hair while massaging his temples to relieve his headache. Then he barked a question to McIlvride: *"Is your fathometer working?"*

"Not clear, repeat again."

"Is your fathometer operable?"

"It's working but not accurately."

"I suggest you take your lead line out and sound the bottom and find

out what your depth is. If you have shallow enough water or water that will hold your anchor, I suggest you throw it over. Let me know before you do."

"Roger."

Just as before, the crew was reluctant to throw the anchor over. "We did not want to drop anchor so close to safety, nor did we want to tie up to any buoy," says McIlvride. "We wanted to get the hell in on our own." They held off on sounding the bottom, which would have been near impossible with the boat rolling and pitching, and instead continued plowing west as slowly as possible. Luckily, they were never faced with the choice of directly disobeying their commander: "The radar came back a little," says McIlvride, "maybe from less snow clutter since we had some protection now that we were well inside the sound and hugging the north shoreline."

"We have our radar back at this time," radioed McIlvride. *"We are attempting to navigate into Beverly Harbor."*

This was the best news Paradis had had all night, and the relief was clear in his voice: *"Ahhh, am I to assume you are a little out of jeopardy and are seeing your way clear?"*

"That's a roger. For the time being. As long as we have radar, I'm going to try to work my way into the harbor."

A couple minutes later, Paradis questioned McIlvride: *"Is your radar still functioning?"*

"That's a Charlie," McIlvride affirmed.

"I want you to head into Beverly."

Just as Paradis completed this sentence, Frank came on the

radio and addressed Paradis. In a calm, matter-of-fact voice, Frank said, *"Pilot boat Can Do."*

Paradis responded, *"Pilot boat Can Do, this is Gloucester Station, over."*

"I have to turn around. My radar went out for some reason, plus the AM antenna. That went overboard with a big crash. So if I can get turned around, I'll be a while getting back. I've got no radar to work with, so I'll be taking it slow."

"Roger, Frank. Probably a good idea to call us in fifteen minutes."

"If I don't get back to you, give me a call. We're going to be busy here for a while."

Paradis must have thought he was caught in a nightmare he couldn't wake up from. First the *Global Hope* issued the Mayday, then his Forty-Four was almost lost, and now Frank was somewhere off Baker's Island without radar. Although Frank's voice made losing the radar sound like no big deal, both he and Paradis knew they had a serious problem. All Frank had now was a compass for navigation. Without radar, however, he had no landmarks to determine his speed or exactly where he was. He could not simply head west toward land because the waves would slam him into the granite shoreline. And when he turned around to head back to Gloucester, he was running into seas that might be moving faster than the boat, effectively negating any forward movement. His control panel may have indicated the propellers were doing ten knots, but that means nothing when seas are twenty feet and screaming along.

The only meaningful position was his last radar fix, which indicated the *Can Do* was just to the northeast of Baker's Island. If he could stay north of Baker's, there was plenty of deep water, but if he got pushed near the island or just to the south of it, he would be in a maze of ledges, which would sink the boat as these ledges had sunk dozens upon dozens of others.

~

Baker's Island and Great Misery Island, separated by a mile, stand guard at the entrance to Salem Sound, with a narrow shipping channel running between them. Although the granite islands are similar in size—approximately a half mile long—Baker's has summer homes and a fifty-nine-foot granite conical lighthouse occupied by a keeper, while Great Misery is uninhabited. In the summer, they are welcome sights for pleasure boaters returning to home port after long trips to Boston, Cape Cod, or north to New Hampshire. And at night the lighthouse, known as Baker Island Light, is especially welcoming, serving as one of the few illuminated navigation aids in the region, marking the approach to Salem Harbor. However, on fog-shrouded nights and in snowy conditions, mariners without radar want to stay far away from the lighthouse and the jagged granite shoreline of the island. The sound of its air horn on a foggy night, particularly if it blasts from a close proximity, sends shivers up the spines of even the most seasoned mariners.

Despite the presence of lighthouses, Baker's Island and the

bare rock slabs known as the Gooseberry Islands, located just south of Baker's, have sunk many vessels. It's as if these islands conspire with the myriad of submerged ledges to form a maze of hull-busting traps. One such accident was caused as much by man's creations as by the elements and the rocky islands. For many years, there were two lights at Baker's Island, but they were replaced by a single light in 1816, and no one told Captain Osgood of the cargo ship *Union,* which was returning to the port of Salem during a heavy snow squall the following year. Seeing only one light where he thought there should be two, Osgood became confused, and the *Union* smashed into the ledge of rock at the northwest side of the island. The crew abandoned ship, and all made it safely to the island, but the *Union* was lost. (Its figurehead, however, was salvaged, and it can still be seen, now mounted atop a home on Norman Street in Marblehead. The two lighthouses on Baker's Island have been replaced by a lone lighthouse at the island's northern end.)

Other crews who ran aground near Baker's were not as lucky as the men aboard the *Union.* The little schooner *Lady Antrim* apparently ran aground at night near Tinkers Island, just south of Baker's, killing all three aboard, in 1710. Like so many wrecks where there are no survivors, we will never know exactly what happened, but judging from the small bits of debris that washed up along Marblehead, it appeared the vessel ran aground and then was torn apart by the waves. The two crew members' bodies washed ashore, but the captain's body was never found.

As Frank's situation on the *Can Do* was worsening, McIlvride's was getting better with each passing moment. Not long after Frank had said he'd lost his radar, the Forty-Four's radar started to clear, and McIlvride spotted a familiar buoy outside Beverly Harbor.

He radioed Paradis that he had spotted the buoy, adding, *"We believe we have the problem solved."*

Paradis responded, *"Calm down, now. Assure yourself you are following the channel."*

"Roger—we believe we are navigating pretty good."

"Give me a call every five minutes, every five minutes, over."

Paradis then radioed Warren to make sure he knew the Forty-Four was in the vicinity of Beverly Harbor. Warren replied, *"Roger, sir, we have several units along the shoreline that are watching the Forty-Four, and we'll bring him into Beverly Harbor Marina."*

Tom Desrosiers remembers that once the crew found the buoy, they knew they were safe. "We tied up at the Jubilee Yacht Club. Later, I remember looking at the propellers of our boat: They were folded over, almost like a squashed tin can. And everything that could be stripped off the boat from the waves was gone— life rings, wooden boat hooks, drop pump canister, you name it."

Six-foot-seven-inch Bob Krom recalls being dog tired and bone cold from the ordeal but, above all, just plain relieved once he stepped on land. As a nineteen-year-old seaman, he'd seen more life and death action in a single evening than most Coast Guard men and women see in their entire careers. Yet even after the blizzard, Krom had another brush with death on the Forty-Four when he was qualifying for the Coast Guard designation known as "Bar Conditions." He was doing his qualifying drills at the mouth of the Merrimack River in Newburyport, where sandbars, the outgoing river, and incoming waves create treacherous, boiling seas when the wind is howling out of the northeast. These were the conditions present when Krom was at the wheel of the Forty-Four. To help stabilize the boat and slow its descent on the downside of the huge waves, a drogue or sea anchor was set behind the boat. At the time, the drogue used was a canvas tube with a wide wire mouth where the water entered; it exited at a narrower opening in the back. The drogue was attached to the boat by a hundred feet of nylon rope.

"There were twenty-foot breakers," says Krom, "and we had just finished doing man-overboard drills when we were heading into the river mouth in following seas. We rode a few waves, and the boat was handling nice. Then we came down the face of a particularly large wave when I heard a loud pop!" The line to the drogue had parted, and without its drag, Krom felt the boat accelerate as it raced downward, and he watched in horror as the Forty-Four's nose buried itself in the trough below. Then he felt the motion of the stern of the boat coming right over his head. All he had time to do was grab a bite of air and hold on to the wheel. The boat had flipped in a shallow area, and sand was churning all around it. Krom described the experience as like being in a giant washing machine with the water pulling at him with a terrific force. He was afraid his last gulp of air wasn't enough, because the boat's mast got caught in the sand and he was upside down for thirty terrible seconds. Finally the mast came free, and the Forty-Four rolled over to the port side, now pointed back out to sea. More big breakers were bearing down on Krom, so he punched the engine into gear and shot out through the waves into deeper water. Of the four people on board, incredibly, the only injury sustained was a broken nose to one of the crew members.

Krom had just pitchpoled—the weight of the seas had held the bow down, and the following wave lifted the stern and flipped the boat end over end. In the history of the Coast Guard, this was only the second time a forty-four had pitchpoled. Krom owed his survival to the fact that he and the others on board were wearing surf belts clamped to the boat. Without the harnesses, they would have been drowned by the waves, crushed by the boat, or shredded by the propellers.

Like many men in the Coast Guard, Krom loved the sea, despite the risks, and found work on the ocean even after leaving the Coast Guard. When Krom was twenty-two, he became a crew member aboard the *Sea Star*, working with Peter Brown (the son of Bob Brown, who owned the *Andrea Gail*, the boat made famous in the book and film *The Perfect Storm*). The *Sea Star* was a seventy-two-foot steel-hulled boat that fished for lobster out on Georges Bank. "It would take us eighteen hours just to reach Georges Bank, and then we would stay there and fish for four or five days. Peter Brown was a very good captain, always monitoring the weather. I fished on the *Sea Star* for a year, and we saw some nasty weather but never anything remotely approaching the seas we experienced in the blizzard."

~

When Bob McIlvride stepped off the Forty-Four, he remembers, that was the first time the gravity of their situation hit him. He had been so busy on the boat he didn't have time to think that he might not make it. It wasn't until one of his crew confided that he'd been praying on board that McIlvride reflected just how close they had come to being killed.

McIlvride also recalls that within minutes of their securing the Forty-Four at Jubilee Yacht Club, the wind ripped the cleats right out of the dock, and they had to tie the boat with several lines to the pilings on the pier. Paradis sent two vehicles down to the yacht club, one a camper driven by fellow Coastie J. R. Murray, who had the unlucky assignment of guarding the Forty-Four alone for the next few days.

The crew began the long drive back to Gloucester. The wind had started drifting the snow, and just minutes after a section of road was plowed, it was covered again. McIlvride was happy he wasn't skippering the car—he left that to Tom Desrosiers because he was from Maine and had the most experience driving in snow.

On the ride back, McIlvride thought of the *Can Do* out there alone in the dark, storm-whipped seas: "I thought the *Can*

Do would make it because Frank and Bucko had been through so much. And unlike our boat, the bridge of the *Can Do* was enclosed. To me, Frank was the original 'old man and the sea,' and seemed to have done it all. If anyone could make it, he could."

PART II

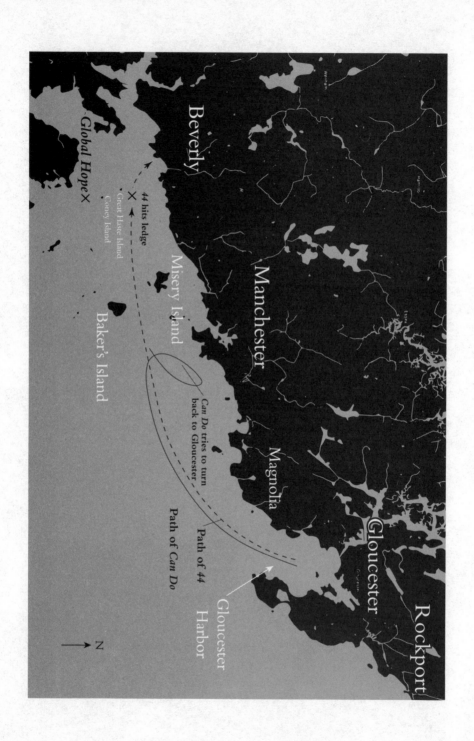

Global Hope X

Beverly

44 hits ledge
X
Great Hasie Island
Coney Island

Manchester

Misery Island

Baker's Island

Magnolia

Can Do tries to turn
back to Gloucester

Path of 44

Gloucester

Gloucester
Harbor

Path of Can Do

Rockport

N

A FAMILY'S ANXIOUS
WAIT

If you were a crew member on a boat at night without radar off Salem Sound and you could choose any captain in the world to pilot that boat, you'd be hard-pressed to choose a better captain than Frank Quirk. Quirk had made the run from Gloucester to Salem and back again hundreds of times in all conditions. Equally important, he stayed calm under pressure, as many mariners from the Gloucester area will attest.

Don Lavato was a Peabody police officer and neighbor of Frank's, who often helped Frank on piloting jobs when conditions warranted an extra hand. Lavato explained that Frank was very cautious, even at the docks, where he'd walk from bow to stern, port to starboard, to make sure the *Can Do* was shipshape before he started the engine. If conditions were bad, he would ask Lavato to accompany him for extra safety, because once the pilot left the *Can Do,* Frank was alone. His concern also helped the pilot, says Lavato: "I remember one time in bad weather the pilot started climbing up the tanker's ladder and slipped. I was standing right below, and I was actually able to catch him and break his fall—if the pilot had landed in the water between us and the tanker he would have been crushed. I was out with Frank in some pretty rotten weather at night. He always stayed cool and seemed to have a knack for sizing up a situation. He almost never got mad or frustrated; he just tried to solve the problem."

Frank's love of the sea came from his father, who was in the merchant marines and had traveled the world before starting a plumbing contracting company in Peabody. Frank's brother, John, said that when they were just five and six years old, their father would take the boys exploring in an old rowboat off the Beverly coast. Their dad had a unique way of teaching them how to swim—he'd toss the boys overboard, and they learned fast.

After Frank's stint in the navy, which he thoroughly enjoyed, he returned to Peabody to join the family plumbing business. "He was unbelievable with anything mechanical," says John. "We used to say, 'If Frank can't figure it out, nobody can.' He had this special way of looking at a problem, studying it, then figuring out how it could be solved." But Frank missed being on the sea, and it wasn't long before he started buying boats and taking on side jobs such as replacing moorings and doing underwater salvage, which required diving.

It was through his diving that Frank's relationship with the Coast Guard first blossomed. In the 1970s Station Gloucester did not have a diving unit, and because Frank was a diver, he would volunteer for jobs—without pay. He often got calls from fishing draggers saying, "We've got something in our net and can't raise it." One time, just outside Gloucester Harbor, Frank dived down and found a torpedo and depth charge tangled in the trawler's net. When he freed those, the net still wouldn't budge, and he went down again. This time, at the other end of the net, he found a small reconnaissance plane attached to the netting. He cut the net, then towed the plane to an area where the fishing fleet would not ensnare it again.

Other diving adventures included a call from the Coast Guard that a recreational diver was in trouble off the coast not far from where Frank was motoring the *Can Do*. Frank quickly donned his wet suit and scuba tanks, and a Coast Guard helicopter flew to the *Can Do* and lowered its basket nearby in the ocean. Frank swam to the basket, and the helicopter raised him up, transferring him to the diving accident scene. Unfortunately, they were too late; Frank dived down but returned to the surface with a lifeless body.

Over the years, Frank bought progressively bigger and better built boats, always naming them the *Can Do*. When Frank began piloting, he became good friends with many of the foreign captains of the ships he helped to bring in. When these captains came back into port, they would keep the friendship going by inviting Frank onto their ship for breakfast or dinner. The captains all liked Frank, not only for his good-natured manner but also because the *Can Do* could help their ships dock. Sometimes the captain would radio down, "Just give us a little push."

Frank's brother, John, remembers Frank for his generosity: "Frank helped me when I was looking for a house on the North Shore just before I was going to be married. One day he said, 'Have you ever thought about building?' I answered that buying land was expensive. And he said, 'Well, I've got a lot, and it's yours. Consider it a wedding gift.' The lot was part of his own land where his house was. He just subdivided it and gave it to me. He then helped me clear the land, pour the foundation, and build the house."

In 1972 Frank became a full-time pilot boat operator, giving up his plumbing wrenches to buy the forty-nine-foot *Can Do*. His business grew fast, and he was soon on-call seven days a week, twenty-four hours a day, sometimes handling five ships a day. His typical job started with a call from a shipping agent, letting him know what time the ship would be approaching one of the harbors. Frank would call the pilot, and the pilot would drive to the *Can Do*. The ship would arrive outside the harbor and hold position two or three miles beyond the harbor's entrance. Frank would then ferry the pilot out to the ship, assisting in its guidance into port by spotting the buoys that marked the channel and communicating this information back to the pilot by radio. Most of the ships were of foreign origin, often with a cargo of coal or oil. Sometimes the captains did not have a good command of English, yet another reason—besides the shoals and ledges—that a local pilot was needed to work in conjunction with Frank.

Both his sons, Frank III and Brian, assisted their father during summers and on weekends and enjoyed their time on the *Can Do* while learning the trade. "Dad was a perfectionist," says Frank III, "but he didn't get on you when you made mistakes. He was very patient. He had great trust in me because he knew I paid attention to detail. Under his supervision, I was guiding four-hundred-foot ships into port when I was just seventeen. Dad wasn't just my father but my friend. We were very close. I could talk about anything with him because we were together so much working on the boat."

Frank told friends he respected the sea but didn't fear it. He knew there was inherent danger in his work and his rescue involvement, but he also knew, from recent experience, danger could find you anywhere, not just on the ocean. On the day of the blizzard, when he was at the Cape Ann Marina with Gard Estes, he told his friend about a car accident he'd had a week earlier. His big Cadillac El Dorado went skidding on a sheet of ice and crashed into a bridge abutment and was totaled. He surprised Gard by offering a piece of introspection he rarely showed: "Gard, I don't know why I'm alive. When I saw that concrete abutment coming at me, I said, 'I'm all done.' I shouldn't be here now."

Gard says he is haunted by those words, coming just a few hours before the *Can Do* went into the blizzard.

~

Audrey Quirk did not begrudge her husband his time away from home, nor was she jealous of his attachment to the *Can Do* and the sea. She, like Frank, was smart enough to adapt, and from early on, she figured if Frank couldn't be home very often, she'd go to the *Can Do*. With kids in tow, that's just what she did every weekend, even in the winter. While Frank would head out to a freighter, Audrey would be in the galley cooking up a pot of fish chowder or preparing lobster.

In warm weather, when no piloting jobs were scheduled, the family would take the *Can Do* out to islands for picnics, swimming, or diving for lobsters. Often they'd motor under the drawbridge and up the canal connecting Gloucester Harbor to the Annisquam River. They might stop at the Cape Ann Marina to see friends who worked there.

When Frank's daughter, Maureen, got married and Frank III joined the marines, their places on the boat were filled by family friends such as young Mark Gelinas or Fred Delourchry, now known as Uncle Fred since helping in the Michael Almeida rescue at the state pier. Occasionally Charlie Bucko; Chief Brad Willey and his wife, Betty; and Dave Curley would come on board for an outing, as well as Maureen's new family. Frank III was not forgotten, and the family would use a tape recorder to make tapes of recent events and send them to the young marine stationed in far-off Okinawa, Japan.

On one tape Frank tells his son that he had seventy piloting trips in January and describes how he pulled a disabled boat off the rocks at Coney Island Ledge in Salem Sound (the very ledge the *Global Hope* would hit). In the background, gulls and terns squawk and cry, giving the recording a real touch of home. On another tape he lets young Frank know who's on board: "Your mother's here making chow, and Brian and Uncle Fred are off running errands. Brian bought a Honda motorcycle and already had his first flat. About the only news to report is that the *Decisive* brought in a Russian trawler caught within the two-hundred-mile limit." He then offers Frank III congratulations on his promotion to lance corporal, adding, "Keep up the good work. I'm very proud of you. Well, this is dear old Dad signing off."

~

Frank III was still in Okinawa the night of the blizzard, which is unfortunate, because he would have been a real comfort to the rest of the family, who were in an agonizing wait for the *Can Do* to return to Gloucester. Maureen remembers how she was working at Mello's Bakery the afternoon of the storm but left early when the snow started to pile up. From her apartment she called her mother to see if everyone got home okay, and Audrey explained that "Dad went out to help the Coast Guard." Maureen didn't think anything of it, because her father was always working with the Coast Guard. She put on her CB radio and listened to her father converse with Paradis, and as the storm worsened, she began to become concerned. Maureen wanted to be with her mother and younger brother, Brian, but the streets were impassible, so instead she called Audrey every half hour and told her everything was going to be fine.

For Audrey, the waiting must have seemed an eternity. Throughout history, the wives of mariners have waited for their safe return. But Audrey's predicament was the exact opposite of that of those women who have to face the unknown. Audrey knew exactly what was happening on the boat, and this added a more intense concern—as if she were on the boat with Frank but unable to do a damn thing to help him. Since Warren Andrews telephoned her at Frank's request— *"call my base and advise her that I won't be in touch for a while"*—Audrey had been sitting in Frank's home office with Brian, both glued to the radio. She was surrounded by all the things Frank cherished, including his nautical books, artifacts found while diving, and photos of himself and her on board all the earlier *Can Do*s. On the door of his office was the original wheel from the current *Can Do*. She tried to stay calm for Brian, reminding him how resourceful Frank was and that with Charlie on board it was almost like having two Franks piloting the boat. Even when she heard the devastating news that Frank had lost his radar, she tried to stay positive, but the shrieking wind outside the house served as a constant reminder that this was no ordinary storm.

There had been several minutes of radio silence since Frank's last transmission to Paradis before Warren Andrews, at about ten P.M., could no longer take the suspense and radioed the *Can Do*: *"How far out were you when you turned around?"*

"I'm not quite sure. We've got problems here without the radar, and everything else is down, just about. We're banging our way up to Gloucester."

At least this response showed that Frank had successfully turned the boat 180 degrees from a southwest bearing into the northeast, no mean feat in hurricane-force wind and waves. He would have had to time his turn in the trough between two waves and complete it before the next wave crested on the boat. If the turn had been incomplete and the *Can Do* was broadside when the next wave hit, it would have capsized under a mountain of frigid, rampaging sea.

THE SEA'S FIRST VICTIMS

Audrey Quirk was not the only wife agonizing over radio transmissions, wondering if the ocean would claim her husband. Just thirty-five miles south of the Quirks' Peabody home, Ellen Fulton was anxiously monitoring the rescue efforts of her husband, Herb, along the shoreline of Scituate, Massachusetts.

Huge waves, coupled with the astronomically high tide, had deluged coastal communities such as Scituate, cutting off many oceanfront homes from higher ground. In some homes the people trapped inside were in danger, as walls and roofs collapsed under the onslaught of wind and surging seas. As in Revere, those caught in homes close to shore were terrified by the staccato bursts of small rocks cast up by the waves and peppering their homes' walls. "Sounded like a machine gun," said a Scituate resident. "We were afraid if we stayed in the house the walls would crumble and we might not have a chance to get away from the rising sea."

Fleeing by foot, however, was not an option, and residents had to wait until police and fire department personnel could evacuate them using small rowboats and skiffs. Herb Fulton, a call captain with the Norwell Fire Department (a neighboring town of Scituate's), was asked to help in the rescues. His wife, Ellen, begged him to stay home, pointing out he was needed right in his own town. "I pleaded with him not to go down there, because I had this feeling something was going to happen. But he went anyway, so I sat by the fire radio, listening to what they were doing."

Arriving at the coast around eleven thirty P.M., Herb and other firemen waded along oceanfront streets, dragging a fourteen-foot aluminum skiff behind, going from house to house to check if anyone was trapped inside. Occasional lightning flashes illuminated the swirling snow, giving the night an eerie hue. A little after midnight, as conditions worsened, Herb was called to Jericho Road, which goes out to Lighthouse Point, a small peninsula of land that separates Scituate Harbor from the ocean. Thundering waves crashed over the seawalls covering a section of Jericho Road. Over the course of the evening, the swale of water expanded, turning Lighthouse Point into an island that faced the full fury of the howling gale.

When Herb arrived on the scene, he was met by several

Scituate firefighters. They gathered on the lee side of a fire truck so they could be heard. A Scituate fire captain shouted that two of their rescue boats and crew had already paddled across to Lighthouse Point but had not been heard from in forty-five minutes. The fire captain requested that Herb and nineteen-year-old volunteer fireman Brian McGowan accompany two Scituate firefighters to check on the missing crews. The four men carried the Norwell skiff down to the water, paddled it across the flooded area, then beached the boat on dry land. They soon found the missing firefighters, who were still knocking on doors, asking residents if they wanted to leave. Herb and Brian assisted in this effort, stopping at the home of Sally Lanzikos.

Sally had been waiting in her home with her five-year-old daughter, Amy, for several hours, wondering if help would ever arrive. The electricity and heat had gone dead about four o'clock, and the surf was coming over the seawall as if it weren't there. Sally recalls how the waves went right over the roof of the two-story house facing the ocean across the street, and that's when she called the fire department.

Sally packed a suitcase for herself and Amy, then stood by the door with a candle, growing more alarmed by the roaring wind that was shaking her house. When help did not arrive, she called the fire department again, and they said they would be there as soon as possible. "About nine o'clock," says Sally, "water started coming in through our kitchen window. Outside I could see the house across the street breaking apart. I stayed by the door with the candle because I was afraid the rescuers might miss us."

While going house to house, Herb and Brian saw Sally's candle, and they went to her aid. The blasting wind was so strong Herb decided to carry Amy, and the group trudged through the blinding snow and knee-deep water back to the boats. As they walked, Sally stared in disbelief at boulders the size of compact cars strewn along the roadway, flung there by the sea. Upon reaching the boats, they joined with others who were waiting to make the crossing. Passengers and rescuers split into groups of from four to six, and Sally, Amy, Herb, and Brian were joined by a couple in their sixties, Mr. and Mrs. Edward Hart. This group boarded the Norwell skiff, with Brian rowing and Herb using a pike pole to push along from the stern. In the confusion Amy was seated in the bow with Mr. Hart while Sally and Mrs. Hart sat in the stern.

About halfway across the flooded area, the group saw a man signaling with a flashlight from a porch of a nearby house surrounded by water. Deciding to help him, they turned the boat toward the man. Then catastrophe struck. A portion of the seawall facing the harbor collapsed, and water that had been trapped inside raced out, like a raging river that had breached a dam. "It was churning white water," says Sally, "and all of the sudden, the boat was flying toward the broken seawall and the harbor."

Brian tried to stop the boat by using an oar against a submerged car, and Herb attempted to hook a telephone pole with his pike pole. The current was too strong, though, and the skiff went careening into the side of a house. The jolt knocked Amy out of the boat and into the frigid waters. Mr. Hart immediately leaned over to grab the girl, and that motion caused the boat to capsize in the dark, swirling vortex. Water was being sucked out to the harbor, taking the six struggling victims with it. "I grabbed Amy several times," says Fulton, "but the current tore her loose. On the way out into deep water, I tried several times to stand but found myself pushed out into water over my head."

All six people in the water were now battling the waves, current, and ice in the darkness of the harbor. Herb's strength was ebbing, and he thought, *This is the end.* He decided to float rather than fight the current, and when he found an area where the flow wasn't too strong, he swam for shore. Finally he reached a shallow area and struggled to safety. Slowly making his way along the beach, he came upon Mrs. Hart, who was still floundering in the water. Dressed in heavy winter clothing, she could not claw her way out, so Herb grabbed her.

While Herb and Mrs. Hart reached dry land, Sally and Mr. Hart were being swept deeper into the harbor. "When the boat capsized, my leg became entangled in a rope hanging from the boat," says Sally. "The boat just dragged me out into the harbor, and I remember screaming for Amy. I thought, *This can't be happening.* Then I had this terrible flash in my mind that my parents were reading a newspaper headline saying they found my body. Maybe that gave me the push to act. I reached down and freed my leg from the rope. That's when I felt Mr. Hart grab my neck from behind. He was drowning. It was awful, but somehow my emotions became detached, and I was able to think clearly—I needed to live to find Amy. I asked Mr. Hart to let go, telling him we'd do better by ourselves, and he did."

Sally considered whether or not she should stay with the boat, but within seconds, an extremely strong gust caught the boat, and she watched it flip end over end, skimming away across the harbor. She saw a post nearby and swam for it, but it turned out to be nothing more than flotsam. Although she didn't feel the icy water, hypothermia was sapping her strength, and the next few minutes were critical for survival. Treading water—expending extra energy because her winter clothes were weighing her down—Sally got her first break when there was a lull in the snowfall, briefly allowing her to see a house onshore.

"It was odd how my mind seemed to process things for a few seconds—almost like a computer. I wasn't panicked but instead started to swim toward the house. I quickly tired. Then for some strange reason, I thought of John F. Kennedy, and how when he was swimming from PT-109 [his patrol boat during WWII] he floated on his back when he was tired. So I floated on my back to rest a minute and then resumed swimming the rest of the way.

"When I reached the rocks, I crawled up a ways and rested, but I was worried a wave was going to wash me back in. Then I thought of Amy and became frantic, running as best I could, screaming for her. I saw people standing down the shore, and they hollered, 'Stay there.' I didn't know what was happening— I thought about going back into the water to try and find her. A strange thing happened next. A tall man in a parka was at my side, and he just hugged me. I couldn't see his face, and he didn't say a word, but it calmed me for a few seconds and prevented me from going in the water. Then two firemen arrived and the man in the parka was gone. I never found out who ... or what he was."

The people Sally saw standing on the shoreline were police and firefighters, gathered around the lifeless body of Amy.

Herb Fulton, Brian McGowan, Mrs. Hart, and Sally all recovered, at least physically. But Amy died, and Mr. Hart was missing and presumed dead. Three months later, his body was found under the Scituate town pier.

The Blizzard of '78 was destroying lives, and it still hadn't reached its peak.

11

TIME IS THE ENEMY

Although the *Cape George* and the *Decisive* were slowly approaching the vicinity of Baker's Island, where the *Can Do* was lost, they had troubles of their own. The *Decisive* was four times bigger than the *Can Do*, but the power of the seas made its size almost irrelevant. First commissioned in 1968, the *Decisive* had endured the worst of conditions, including a stint in the International Ice Patrol in the North Atlantic, but it had never been battered as on the night of the blizzard. The 210-foot cutter took several rolls in the sixty-degree range. The men on board could only hope the next big roll didn't put it completely on its side at ninety degrees, from which they wouldn't recover. "Picture looking at a wall of water," says Jim Quinn, "which is the size of a three-decker home. That's what it was like with each oncoming wave."

Quinn says that he didn't even have to climb up the stairs from the engine room but instead just time a wave and jump, and the motion of the ship would catapult him to the next level. He knew the *Can Do* was now in trouble, but the *Decisive*'s radar wasn't much good because of all the snow. The men up on the bridge of the cutter only had brief periods at the tops of waves to get a look ahead—most of the time they were surrounded by those walls of water.

Frank and the crew must have surely known that the chances of the *Decisive* or the *Cape George* finding them on the open ocean were so poor it was not even worth hoping for that to happen. Yet Frank continued to remain calm, as was evidenced when Paradis tried to get a fix on his position: *"Pilot boat* Can Do, *how far out were you, Frank, when you lost your radar?"*

"Not quite sure. When the radar went out, I was taking a reading on Baker's Island. When the AM antenna came down, I don't know if it hit the radar on the way down. We're trying to nurse along here, best we can. So can't tell you just where we are right now. Once in a while I'll get a blip on the radar. Trying to make the mouth of the harbor. Hang in there for a few minutes, and I'll give you a better position when I find out where I am."

"Roger. I'd appreciate it if you give me a call every fifteen minutes. If you want, I can send the Forty-One out there to see if they can pick you up on radar."

"Yeah, okay, well, you call me back, 'cause I'm going to be losing

track of time here, so give me a call in fifteen minutes, and we'll let you know how we're making out."

Chief Paradis didn't have a lot of options. The only boat at his disposal was the forty-one footer, the same Forty-One that got beyond the breakwater earlier and had to turn back. He offered its services now because both he and Frank thought the *Can Do* would soon be at the mouth of Gloucester Harbor. However, in just the brief period of time since the *Can Do* left Gloucester, the winds had increased more greatly still, screaming at seventy and eighty miles per hour, and some gusts reached a terrific one hundred miles per hour.

The *Can Do* was going directly into the teeth of these bitter winds wailing out of the northeast. The twenty- and thirty-foot breaking seas were pushing the boat backward faster than it could motor forward. On the way down toward Salem, Frank was going full throttle to give himself a bit of maneuverability in the racing seas. Now, heading into the waves, he needed to find a slower speed to minimize the water taken over the bow. Icing was an additional concern, and the spray was freezing on the deck, rails, and pilothouse. It was essential Frank make forward progress, but he had to do so at a snail's pace, while still keeping approximately a half mile to a mile offshore in deep water. Hugging the shore any closer would put him in jeopardy of striking islands near the mouth of Gloucester Harbor.

The Forty-One did go back out, and on board was Bill Cavanaugh, who had fully recovered from his broken neck injury sustained in the *Chester Poling* rescue. "I was off duty down in Marblehead," says Cavanaugh, "but I still got the call to come to the station. I explained that my car, a Gremlin, would never make it through all the snow, but they said, 'Don't worry; we have it all arranged for you to be brought back up.'" Station Gloucester had lined up a series of snowplows from different towns to transport Cavanaugh back to the station using a relay approach. Each plow would carry him to the northern end of their town line, where the next town's plow would be waiting to continue the relay.

"When I arrived at the station," recalls Cavanaugh, "it looked like it was floating—there was seawater entirely encircling it. I joined the rest of the Forty-One crew, and Paradis instructed us to try and get a radar fix on the *Can Do* from just outside the breakwater. He made it clear, however, that we were not to put ourselves in jeopardy. As soon as we were on board and departed, we knew we were in for a long night. It was a battle just to get to Ten Pound Island within the harbor. Conditions were unbelievable. We hadn't even reached the breakwater and our radar was out. The waves were so big, even with our radar, it wouldn't have helped much, because each time we went down in a trough, the radar would have just picked up the seas in the front and back. Our bow was submerged a good part of the time—we call that green water because it's not just cutting through crests of spray but is actually in the sea. I had learned a lot from when I was a rookie on the *Chester Poling* rescue, and that was to make sure I knew when the waves were going to hit. Most of us, over the course of time, develop a built-in sense of timing so you know when to brace yourself so you're not airborne like I was when I got injured."

Cavanaugh says they made it to the breakwater, but the seas beyond it were breaking, and the twenty- and thirty-foot waves surely would have overwhelmed the utility boat: "The Forty-One wasn't designed for those kinds of seas, and we couldn't get beyond the breakwater without being killed. At that time there was no escape hatch in the Forty-One's enclosed area."

~

Back in Salem, Warren Andrews was dying inside, listening to the *Can Do*'s worsening situation. Frank was not just his friend but more like a brother. Warren had been on the radio with Frank for so many years he sometimes felt as if he were on the boat himself, able to see clearly everything Frank described. He knew Frank had made it through dozens of severe storms, including the one that split the *Chester Poling* in half, yet still there was something different about this night. The combination of snow, incredible winds, and monstrous seas was making this storm a killer, particularly for any boat caught in its grip at night. Warren had heard what was happening on the Coast Guard's largest cutter in the area, and he knew that if the 210-foot *Decisive* was rolling sixty degrees—the deck almost at a right angle to the seas—the *Can Do* must be faring far worse.

Finally Warren couldn't wait any longer, and he broke in on

the radio, concern giving his voice a clipped and tense quality. *"This is Salem Control. Pilot boat* Can Do, *what's the situation?"*

"We've got problems here without the radar and everything else. Boy, I'll tell you it's some wild out here. So we're just poking along. I've got plenty of water. I'm just trying to pick up something to go by."

Charlie Bucko was likely standing—as best he could—by the helm with Frank, hoping to pick something up on the malfunctioning radar. Judging from the comments of the crew of the *Decisive* and the *Cape George*, the two men were already exhausted just from the energy expended trying to keep their balance and from being knocked around. For the other three men on the *Can Do*—Curley, Fuller, and Wilkinson—the return trip was even worse, because they could only hang on and wait.

At this point whatever tasks needed to be done, such as securing any equipment that was jarred loose, would have been completed. Now they could only hope the *Can Do* could struggle back to Gloucester without popping a hatch or splitting a seam—and each wave that pounded the boat made that scenario less likely. If they didn't know it before, they now realized they were in serious trouble. The murderous seas and the howling gale didn't give an inch and instead were trying to claw their way inside the boat and get at the men.

The three men were wedged in a sitting position between the table and the cushioned benches. They were likely seasick and vomiting from the endless rising and falling, as if trapped on a roller coaster that had no off switch. They were totally spent from bracing themselves for each jarring impact the *Can Do* made after cresting a wave. *Pow! Pow! Pow!* they heard over and over.

The men were struggling to push the fear back, keep it in the pit of the stomach, keep it from taking over. They could only pray that Frank would make it to the breakwater and see it before they were slammed into it and crushed. Maybe the thought that they were losing ground and actually going backward toward the shoals of Baker's Island crossed their minds, but it was a thought too terrible to contemplate and best kept to oneself.

Even if they could hear one another above the growling sea and demonic wind, there was nothing to say at this point. Each man was likely lost in his own thoughts, just trying to make it through the next minute. Dave Curley could have been thinking back to that afternoon at the marina. Dave usually only went there at night and almost never in the daytime, because his electrical work took him all over the North Shore. Had he headed home rather than to the marina, he wouldn't be stuck in this heaving black void.

How odd is the nature of life, that one seemingly insignificant decision can set in motion events that spin out of control. Just a few hours earlier, he and his friends were safe and warm, laughing, and maybe even glad for the storm because it gave them a break from the daily grind of work. At that time Dave Curley's biggest immediate worry was whether the drive home would be a long one in the snow. Now, instead of watching the news of the blizzard on TV, he was in it, wondering if the next wave to break on the bow would be the one to bury them.

Commercial fisherman Kenny Fuller knew the toll the punishing waves were taking on the *Can Do*. From his experience fishing far out at sea, he also realized time was their enemy. If they didn't get into the harbor quickly, the vessel would eventually—perhaps piece by piece—succumb to the unrelenting waves. And if a rogue wave hit or a sea slammed them from a slightly different direction, Fuller knew, it could be all over in a matter of seconds. Every fisherman from Gloucester knows someone who didn't make it back after being caught in a storm. Still, it's ironic that Fuller had successfully made dozens of high-risk trips—over a hundred miles offshore searching for bluefin tuna—and now he was in the battle of his life just a mile from the coast.

Facing the possibility of death leads some to contemplation, and Kenny Fuller might have thought what a rough couple of years he'd had. Before trying his hand at fishing, he owned the Patio Restaurant in Rockport, but mounting debt, some from his gambling habit, forced him to sell. Friends said Fuller had a bigger problem than gambling: his own generosity. "He was too good-hearted to be a businessman," says Gard Estes. "Any friend that came to the restaurant would have drinks and food on the house. And just about everybody was his friend."

If Fuller wasn't cut out for business, Wilkinson was the exact opposite, using his shrewd management skills to increase profits at the Cape Ann Marina and the Captain's Bounty Motor Lodge.

As dedicated as Wilkinson was to his job, he took time out for his children, a daughter and two sons. "My father could be demanding," says his son Donald Jr., "but he cared about us kids and put us first. Two or three times a week we had 'game night,' where we would each take turns choosing what game we were going to play together. Dad always picked Monopoly, and of course usually won."

Wilkinson's business savvy and outgoing personality attracted friends and connections all over the state. "If somebody was being treated unfairly," says Gard, "Don would make a few calls and straighten things out. Of course we never called him Don—his nickname was Uncle Al, because we thought he looked like the Boston Strangler, Albert DeSalvo."

If business was Wilkinson's talent, his passion was powerboat racing. Wilkinson competed in powerboat racing and sponsored charity races to benefit the Lions Club Eye Research Program. A photo in a 1977 edition of the *Gloucester Times* shows a smiling Wilkinson pumping his fist from the cockpit of a powerboat after he won a race in rough seas off Gloucester. Not all the participants of the race, however, were smiling at the end. During that race, one boat sank and two men were hospitalized. Speeding at seventy miles per hour, their boat slewed sideways, pitching one contestant thirty feet in the air and slamming the other into the boat's superstructure, smashing the vertebrae in his back in the process. At the finish line was the *Can Do*, and Frank helped get the men to safety before they drowned.

Gard Estes summed up the five men as the best of friends, always together: "We were family, and like family, there wasn't anything we wouldn't do for each other." And now there was nothing the friends could do for one another except keep their emotions in check and silently pray.

HEADING NORTHEAST

While Frank and Charlie tried to inch northeastward, the ninety-five-foot *Cape George* had finally reached the outskirts of Salem Sound. At approximately eleven P.M., Paradis asked them for a status report on their position and their radar's effectiveness. The *Cape George* responded, but Skipper Glen Snyder's voice could barely be heard above the howling wind: *"Negative on the loran and navigation. We think we are three miles southwest off Marblehead. Making four knots. Wind is blowing sixty-two knots. Seas about twenty feet. We're taking a real beating out here. Lost fathometer."*

Paradis replied, *"Be advised the Forty-Four ran aground and is presently tied up in Beverly. We don't know how much damage she sustained on the bottom. She lost her radar and fathometer, and she couldn't navigate. The tanker is aground, but we do not have a good position on her."*

"Is there any assistance to her at this time?"

"Negative. There is no assistance on scene."

"Is there any chance of that tanker breaking up?"

"We do not know at this time. As far as we know all POBs are on board and they're okay, but we do not know for sure; all we know is the tanker is aground."

In Boston, Jim Loew was monitoring this exchange. This was the same Jim Loew who had skippered the cutter that saved several men from the *Chester Poling*. Now he was a Rescue Coordination Center (RCC) controller for the First Coast Guard District in Boston, which covered an area from the Maine–Canada border south to the Rhode Island–Connecticut border and offshore. Jim had the watch for RCC that night, and it was he who sent the *Cape George* out when he learned that the *Global Hope* was in trouble.

"It was tough," says Lowe, "to send the *Cape George* out into that storm, because I knew exactly how dangerous it would be for them. But the vessel had a good skipper in Glen Snyder, and he knew that I had 'been there' with the *Cape George,* and he trusted my judgment that we needed him to go out on this mission. If the *Global Hope* was sinking, we were going to need more than the patrol boats that went out from Gloucester. Glen knew he'd be entering unpredictable conditions. Before setting out, he took the extraordinary, but prudent, measure of 'setting material condition ZEBRA,' requiring all watertight doors, hatches, fittings (except those needed for ventilation) to be closed and kept closed."

This proved a wise decision, because without navigation equipment, the cutter was in increasing peril as it approached the ledge-filled waters of Salem Sound. Seaman apprentice Vern DePietro was on the bridge, watching his superiors discuss where they might be. "Myron was studying the charts," says DePietro, "trying to memorize where the hazards were located. His memory saved our bacon, because just a few minutes later, we took water in the bridge, and the charts turned into mush, so we had nothing to go by. Things were getting pretty tense, but I kept my mouth shut."

~

Loew learned the latest news from the *Cape George*'s first class boatswain's mate, Dennis Hoffer, because Snyder was so busy. Besides the lost radar and charts, Hoffer reported, they had no high-frequency radio, the anemometer (wind speed/direction gauge) wasn't registering, and they had zero visibility. Hoffer then gave Loew his loran-C readings and asked if he could plot their position and provide them a course to both Salem Sound and Gloucester. Loew did so and then decided he had heard enough. He released them from the case and told them to get to safety, basically making it their option to attempt to proceed to Gloucester or turn around and reenter Boston Harbor. Snyder chose to avoid the danger of turning and decided to continue north-northeast for Gloucester.

In Gloucester, Paradis was cursing the tanker captain. If only the *Global Hope*'s captain had checked his position when he was first asked if he was dragging anchor, none of this would have been happening. The captain could have set an additional anchor, added more ballast, or started up his engines and held his position with his bow into the wind. Instead he did nothing and later cried that he was taking on water, which set in motion all the events that followed.

Paradis now had new worries about the *Cape George*. He knew that if the *Cape George* was without navigational aids, they wouldn't be able to locate the *Can Do* or the *Global Hope*. And if it turned out that the *Global Hope* had broken apart and there was loss of life, every newspaper and politician in the region would be asking why the Coast Guard wasn't able to do what they were supposed to do: save lives. Every decision Paradis made would be analyzed later, when hindsight would be twenty-twenty.

Now, however, his immediate task was to get the *Can Do* to safety. He radioed Frank and again asked if he had any idea where he might be.

Frank responded, *"Position unknown at this time. Radar's down. We're trying to stay offshore and find the entrance to Gloucester. It is some howling out here and not having any luck."*

"Roger, if you would like an escort we'll be standing by."

"Okay. If your radar is on, you might try to pick us up outside the harbor. We have nothing to work with, and we are just trying to fish around at the present."

"Roger, if you want an escort we'll be standing by at this time."

"Okay, roger."

"We'll see if we can pick you up on radar, and maybe you'll see the blue light."

What both men knew, though it went unsaid, was that this scenario was a long shot. The Forty-One was battling to hold position at the entrance to Gloucester Harbor, and the only way they were going to be able to pick up the foundering pilot boat on radar was if it made it to the breakwater.

IN SHOAL WATERS

At midnight the storm was merciless in its pelting fury. Both wind and seas had continued to increase. Beyond the windshield of the *Can Do,* driving foam, spray, and snow filled the frigid night sky. Each time the *Can Do* crested a wave, its propeller was momentarily out of the water, whining crazily, and the boat was out of Frank's control. Then down the wave it plunged, as if going over a cliff. At the bottom of the trough, green water engulfed the bow before cascading off as Frank coaxed the pilot boat up the next wave. Every few minutes he was punched by a confused sea coming at the *Can Do* from a slightly different angle. Frank was like a blindfolded fighter thrust into the ring against an unseen opponent who threw all haymakers and no jabs.

The force of a thirty-foot wave is almost unimaginable, considering that just one cubic foot of water weighs more than sixty-two pounds, and one cubic yard of water weighs nearly seventeen hundred pounds. To the men on the *Can Do*, each wave felt as if a gigantic battering ram were being slammed into the foundering boat, intent on busting it open. As February 6 ended and February 7 began, it seemed like the storm picked the *Can Do* as its target and was trying to stop the boat before it could reach its home port.

The *Can Do*, however, was a rugged boat, and Frank had made many improvements to it. On its modest-size front windshield, he installed a visor to reduce the glare on sunny days. For snow and sleet, he mounted a small motorized revolving circular plate of glass on the main windshield, which helped keep that portion free of ice and snow for better visibility.

Frank also wanted to be sure other boats could see him in low light. Just below the wheelhouse, he painted a large section bright orange and upon that wrote the word PILOT in big black letters on the far left and right, with the boat's name in the middle. The hull was black, the superstructure light gray, and the exhaust stack red. A stainless steel rail went around the hull. For extra safety, Frank added stanchion pipes that supported a thick safety cable that encircled the entire boat. The radio and radar antennae stretched skyward off the back of the pilothouse, and flying above those was an American flag. Inside the boat, Frank had stowed several pieces of safety and rescue equipment, including a ten-man life raft, fire extinguishers, first-aid kits, and wet suits.

The *Can Do's* low superstructure both helped and hurt its chances of survival during the blizzard. It gave the vessel a low center of gravity, which aided in stability against the powerful wind gusts. But the low superstructure also meant the exhaust stack was not far from the ocean's surface, leaving it vulnerable to a deluge of water from a monstrous wave. And the longer the boat stayed out in the storm, the greater the probability that something would fail. Each man on board knew it was imperative to immediately find that entrance to Gloucester Harbor. Judging from the previous radio communication, when Frank radioed Paradis to have the forty-one-footer try to pick them up on radar, the crew of the *Can Do* believed they were getting closer to safety. After that communication, little more was said, and Frank put all his focus on feeling his way up each wave while keeping his bow pointed north-northeast.

Suddenly, at approximately one A.M., a different voice came over the radio from the *Can Do*. It was Charlie Bucko.

"Gloucester Station, Can Do, *Gloucester Station,* Can Do.*"*

At Station Gloucester, a lower-level officer had temporarily relieved Chief Paradis from the communications room, and this man quickly responded, *"Roger. This is Gloucester Station."*

Charlie Bucko, in a remarkably clear and calm voice, then said, *"Roger. This is not a drill; this is not a drill . . . a Mayday, a Mayday, a Mayday. Over."*

"Roger, pilot boat Can Do, *this is Gloucester; we have you at this time."*

There was a long pause, and nothing more was heard from the *Can Do.*

Station Gloucester shouted, "Can Do, *keep sending traffic, over!*"

There was no response. The man at the mike immediately had Paradis summoned back to the communications room, and shortly after his arrival, Charlie came back on the radio, now sounding out of breath:

"Gloucester Station, Can Do, *Gloucester Station,* Can Do.*"

"This is Gloucester Station."

"We're not sure what has happened at this time . . . ah. . . . We feel we may have hit the breakwater [outside the harbor].*"

Charlie paused for three seconds and then shouted, *"Negative on my last, negative on my last!"*

"Roger, do you happen to know approximately where you might be?"

"That's a negative."

There were several anxious seconds of silence; then Paradis, exhausted and tense, responded, *"This is Gloucester Station; keep on talking to us here."*

"Mike, be advised we are in shoal water—" Suddenly, in the background, Frank's angry voice is heard: *"Look, give me that—"* The rest of Frank's words were cut off.

"This is Gloucester Station, over. Keep talking to us. Let us know the situation."

"We're trying to get into deeper water here." The voice was Charlie's again.

"Keep talking."

"We're in shoal water. Our windshield is out. Position unknown. Action extremely violent."

This last message began to explain what had happened. The *Can Do* had hit something in shoal, or shallow, water, either the ocean's bottom or a rock ledge. At the same instant, the windshield was blown out, probably from a giant wave. The wall of water, parts of the windshield, and probably the motor for the spinning window crashed into Frank's head, knocking him from the wheel. Because Charlie was likely standing by the wheel with Frank, he, too, would have been sent reeling backward, arms flailing, by the booming fist of water. The pounding of the seas—which was loud even inside a sealed wheelhouse—was now a deafening roar.

Curley, Wilkinson, and Fuller had all accompanied Frank and Charlie to lend a hand—now they were needed, and then some. They must have been stunned by the wall of water pouring into the boat, but they had to recover immediately or they'd lose the *Can Do* and their lives.

Frank had been temporarily knocked unconscious. That was why Charlie took over the radio and the wheel. When Frank regained consciousness, he wanted to get back to the wheel, despite having cuts on his face and head. While the boat was pitching wildly, Frank struggled toward the radio, trying to regain control of the microphone. One of the crew likely held him for a minute, telling him he was badly injured while trying to stop the flow of blood. Two of the others dashed below and frantically searched for something to seal the jagged opening of the shattered windshield. Each cresting wave was pouring more water into the boat, and the crew only had seconds to hold the sea at bay before it was too late. The two men hauled up a mattress and stuffed it in the gaping hole—it didn't entirely stop the icy water from gaining entry, but it bought them more time to stay afloat.

The actions of the men at that time were crucial to whether or not they would perish in the next moments. Quirk was injured, water had poured through the opening where the windshield once was, and the boat continued to founder in shoal water. Charlie Bucko, relying on instinctive reactions, had only seconds to maneuver the boat into deeper water before it was too late. But the waves he was encountering were much deadlier than those they had been fighting on the open sea.

When waves hit shallow water, they are shortened, become steeper, and break more frequently. These chaotic sea conditions were lifting the *Can Do* up twenty feet only to let it free-fall down and scrape bottom. In seas of this magnitude, the depth of shoal water and the trouble it can cause for boats is relative to wave height. Normally the *Can Do*, which drew six feet of water, had no trouble in sea depths as shallow as ten feet, but the giant waves left a void in their wake, exposing the ocean floor.

Slowly, the options for the men on board the *Can Do* were being taken away.

~

Before the *Can Do* went into its Mayday situation, Gard Estes and Louis Linquata, back at the marina, had decided they had to do something to help. The men had access to a Jeep that was formerly used as a two-seater mail truck. It had a CB radio inside, and they were briefly able to raise Frank on the radio. He'd said, *"We're in deep trouble with no radar,"* then went on to say that he might be near Magnolia Beach and he wanted them to get searchlights there, thinking if worse came to worst, he could try to beach the boat onshore.

Gard and Louis ran back inside the marina and started calling neighboring police and fire departments, civil defense, and friends from the Northeast Surf Patrol, requesting them to head to Magnolia. Their plan was to get as many vehicles as possible down to Magnolia Beach and shine their headlights seaward in the hope that Frank would see the lights and be able to drive the *Can Do* up on the sand.

The two men hopped back in the Jeep and headed south for Magnolia. "I don't know how we got there," says Louis. "The streets were either blocked with drifting snow or flooded. It was almost impossible to see more than a foot or two past our headlights. When we got to Magnolia Beach, we were relieved to see there were several police and civil defense men gathered on a nearby roadway."

By the time they reached the beach, they had heard Charlie's Mayday and knew Frank was hurt. The men parked their cars and trucks as close to the beach as possible and shined their headlights out toward the ocean. Then they broke up into groups of two or three and tried to walk closer to the water, thinking the *Can Do* might have already been smashed in the surf.

Gard explains what happened next: "I had moved toward the ocean and was talking with a police officer when a giant wave crashed over the seawall. It sounded like Logan Airport with jets taking off right next to us. The wave knocked us down and rolled us. As the wave receded, it started to take us with it. We grabbed hold of the seawall. We were literally hanging on by our fingertips. Once the water went past us, we ran like hell. There was a tennis club nearby, and after that wave hit, half of it was gone—it looked like a stick of dynamite had been thrown into it."

Two civil defense men were caught in the same wave but were unable to grab the seawall. Louis, standing just twenty feet away, watched as they disappeared beneath a receding wave. Then seconds later, another breaker hurled the men back up onshore. Louis, Gard, and several others helped them onto their feet, and they all ran to a nearby house. Inside the home, it felt safe until a wave came up and over the roof of the house. Louis and Gard stayed inside for a few minutes but thought the *Can Do* might have been pushed farther south, so they returned to the Jeep. "We headed down toward Beverly," says Gard, "and that little mail carrier got us through many sections of waist-deep water. We stopped at several places such as Hospital Point, looking for the *Can Do*, and even searched for debris from the boat. Then we headed north again, stopping now and then to shine our lights out to sea, but there was no sign of the boat."

Since the original Mayday communications, nothing had been heard from the *Can Do*. Paradis and Warren called the boat over and over, but their queries went unanswered. Charlie's last message rang in their ears like an ill wind: *We're in shoal water. Our windshield is out. Position unknown. Action extremely violent.*

The *Can Do* was a fifty-foot steel pilot boat captained by Frank Quirk.
[Quirk family]

Frank Quirk receives a commendation from the Coast Guard for his
assistance during the rescue of the *Chester Poling*.
[Quirk family]

During the first night of the blizzard, the oil tanker *Global Hope* took on water when its hull was fractured. [United States Coast Guard]

The forty-four-foot motor lifeboat was a rugged, reliable vessel that the Coast Guard used for many functions, including rescues. [USCG]

This photograph illustrates how a pilot boat pulls up alongside a tanker or freighter to let the pilot climb up to the ship.
[Quirk family]

The pilot leaves the pilot boat and climbs aboard the ship to take control for the last mile or two into port.
[Quirk family]

Charismatic and handsome, Charlie Bucko served in the Marines before joining the Coast Guard.
[Bucko family]

Bob McIlvride was the skipper of the Forty-Four.
[Bob McIlvride]

The Forty-Four was a self-righting boat if it capsized, but in the Blizzard of '78, that was little comfort. [USCG]

Access to the engine room on the Forty-Four was through a hatch in the wheelhouse. [Author's collection]

At 210 feet, the *Decisive* was a Coast Guard cutter similar to this one.
[USCG]

Surging waves flattened this home in Kingston, Massachusetts.
[*Boston Herald*]

Fishing boats pushed
atop the broken pier
at Scituate.
[Town of Scituate]

The crashing spray
of waves came almost
to the top of Minot
Light in Scituate.
[Kevin Cole, *Boston Herald*]

Hundreds of cars and motorists were stranded on Route 128.
[Vince Horrigan]

Homes on Stanton Lane in Scituate were demolished.
[Town of Scituate]

The *Can Do*'s radar bar sits atop the pilothouse, where the person is standing.
[Quirk Family]

Mike Paradis, commander of Station Gloucester, was at the radio
set in this room at the station throughout the blizzard.
[USCG]

Frank Quirk was a scuba diver, and sometimes he would help the Coast Guard when they needed a diver.
[Quirk family]

The frozen waters outside Scituate Harbor.
[Author's collection]

The *Cape George* was the same type of cutter shown here.
[USCG]

This circular spinning window was mounted on the main windshield
and would keep the ice from forming. When the windshield broke,
the spinning window and glass hit Frank.
[Quirk family]

Mel Cole had a powerful radio set at his home, and he was the only person who could talk to Frank in the early morning hours.
[Author's collection]

In this model of the *Can Do*, the anchor can be seen on the deck. Somehow, Charlie Bucko was able to get it free from the ice and hurl it overboard.
[Author's collection]

Most of the men on the *Cape George* think a giant wave hurled them up and over the breakwater at Gloucester Harbor. [Author's collection]

Sharon Fish was Charlie Bucko's fiancée.
[Sharon Watts]

Pilot Brian Wallace tried to fly his helicopter to Salem Sound and search for the *Can Do*.
[Brian Wallace]

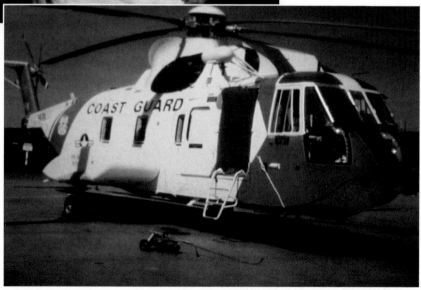

The Jayhawk Coast Guard helicopter flown by Brian Wallace.
[Brian Wallace]

The second story of this home blew off the first story.
[Theodore Atkinson]

The snow was so deep, the only way to clear the streets was with giant front-end loaders. There are cars hidden under the snow.
[Tom Maguire]

The waves caused erosion right up to the foundations of these homes in Plymouth.
[Paul Benoit, *Boston Herald*]

When the *Can Do* was later raised from the bottom of the ocean, all that was left was the hull. Note the gash in the bow.
[Quirk family]

TROUBLES ON THE
CAPE GEORGE

When Charlie Bucko radioed the Mayday, Audrey, Brian, and Maureen Quirk all heard it on their radios at home. Concern turned to terror. The radio transmissions were not clear, but the family knew it wasn't Frank on the mike, and that spoke volumes to the seriousness of the situation. Fifteen-year-old Brian immediately wanted to get down to the Coast Guard station, if only to be closer to his father. But the storm had already dumped a foot and a half of snow, and the roads were virtually impassible. Maureen wanted to be with Brian and her mother, but even though she only lived a couple of miles away, getting to them would not be easy.

In the minutes that followed the Mayday, all communication

with the *Can Do* ceased and the family was aghast. Audrey called Paradis, hoping he was still in communication with the *Can Do*. The commanding officer tried to sound positive, but he had to explain that neither he nor Warren Andrews could raise the boat. Audrey's call was just one of many that were pouring into Gloucester Station from people who had been listening to the drama on their marine radios.

Machinery Technician Ron Conklin was Officer of the Day, working alongside Paradis in the communications room. He recalls that about midnight, "the place became a madhouse. Calls were coming in every minute from family, people wanting to help, and from people who thought they saw the lights of the *Can Do*. Others called saying they thought they heard a boat's engine, and some of these callers were from as far away as Ipswich and Boston. We had ambulances on standby at the police stations, and they were calling to ask if we heard anything more."

Ralph Stevens was a young seaman who was standing by the door of the communications room listening to everything that was happening. He was especially concerned with the situation of the forty-one-footer holding position by the breakwater. Earlier that night, he'd been on board the Forty-One when it aborted its trip to aid the *Global Hope*: "We literally could not see a thing, and the conditions were unbelievable. I remember asking the guys on board, 'What the hell are we trying to do—that huge tanker wasn't going anywhere, and even if we got there, it would be impossible to get anyone off.' So we decided to turn around near Norman's Woe. I'm convinced that had we gone just a little bit further, I would not be here today. So when I heard they sent the Forty-One back out again, I thought, *My God, it's suicide to go back out*. In fact, I had already made the decision that if I was told to go back out, I was going to refuse. Let them court-martial me. Sometimes I think in situations like this, adrenaline takes over, and common sense gets left behind."

For the men standing outside the communications room, the normal flow of time transformed into a surreal zone, as if at half speed. All night they had listened to the *Can Do's* progress, trying to will the pilot boat toward the harbor. And now there were no incoming messages from the boat. Some prayed, and others discussed what might have happened to the pilot boat after its windshield was lost.

Ralph Stevens says that the men in the hallway talked softly so they could hear what was happening in the radio room: "Things were really hopping in there, and we could feel the tension. Paradis was on the radio, a couple other people were on the phones, and another was on the teletype giving situational updates to Boston. The rest of us were just standing in the hall-way, hoping we'd hear Bucko come back on the radio. Charlie Bucko was the guy who taught me how to run a Coast Guard boat, and he was a great instructor. I was hoping somehow he'd get lucky this one time and make it. The guys in the hall were just standing there, anxiously waiting for news. We all knew Charlie and Frank, and we knew things didn't look good."

All this commotion was not helping Mike Paradis. His right-hand man, Brad Willey, was unable to reach the station, trapped by the snows at Annisquam Light, ten miles away. Any kind of help would have been appreciated. From where Paradis sat, he could look out the window into the swirling snow and be reminded of just how limited his resources were. The station's concrete helicopter pad was just a few feet from the window. He must have wished conditions would change so a helo from Coast Guard Air Station Cape Cod at Otis Air Force Base could get airborne.

From time to time, the tall, thin station commander stood up from his chair and rubbed his temples, pushing back his white hair. He'd been handling this crisis for six straight hours, and he needed a break. He probably figured there was a good chance the *Can Do* had capsized, and he wondered if people would blame him for what happened.

Paradis was just months away from retirement, and never in his Coast Guard career had he had a night like this, when almost everything that could go wrong did. He may have thought how cruel and ironic it was that Frank and Charlie, who had answered dozens of Mayday calls, had no one to help them in their time of need. The forty-one-footer could not venture much farther than the breakwater, the Forty-Four was damaged down in Salem, the *Decisive* was still miles away, and the *Cape George* was without effective radar. Still, the station commander hoped that the *Can Do* might get close enough for the forty-one-footer to make radar contact.

Paradis radioed the Forty-One: *"Four-one-three-five-three, this is Gloucester Station. The* Can Do *is in Mayday situation at this time. Where are you?"*

"We are outside the breakwater and no radar contact with the *Can Do*."

Paradis responded as if talking through clinched teeth. *"Get in the best position you can and ride it out."*

"I'll do my best."

Paradis next raised the *Cape George* and asked if they were still heading to Gloucester.

Skipper Glen Snyder shouted back to be heard above the shrieking wind, hesitating between each sentence to be sure he could be heard: *"Station Gloucester, cutter* Cape George, *that's affirmative! We are presently lost! I repeat, we are presently lost! We have lost loran reception. We believe we are two and a half miles east . . . of Cape, of, ah, off, ah, Eastern Point. But we cannot confirm it. We are proceeding toward shore to try and pick up some lights and confirm our position."*

"Do you have any radar?"

"Radar is performing poorly! I can barely pick up any landmasses at all. What I do pick up we are unable to identify."

"Understand that we have the pilot boat Can Do *in a Mayday situation somewhere near Gloucester and Magnolia. We request on your way in to make any sweeps in any area if possible to see if we can pick up the pilot boat."*

Seaman Vern DePietro remembers that conversation as if it happened yesterday: "When I heard Glen Snyder say we were lost, that really scared me, because the seas were still getting bigger. I knew we weren't far from shoal water, and the *Cape George* drew six feet, four inches, aft and about four feet, four inches, forward, so we could have easily hit an unseen shoal."

The *Cape George* and the *Can Do* were not all that far apart, with the *George* just to the south of Baker's Island and the pilot boat to the north. But without functioning radar on either boat, they might as well have been in different oceans. Snyder had to worry about hitting the shoals near Baker's Island. His cutter performed sluggishly, with significant ice buildup causing it to wallow heavily in the pounding seas. Freezing spray hardened as soon as it struck, making the boat top-heavy. Usually when this happened, men were sent on deck with baseball bats to pound and chip away at the ice. That night, however, it was impossible to spend more than a second or two on deck without being swept over.

Executive Petty Officer Myron Verville was concerned about the weight of the ice on the cutter, but it was the ice damage to the radar that really had him worried. He recalls that the radar only worked partially. The *Cape George* also took on so much water some of its electronics shorted out, and the crew was without their primary loran. There was an old loran system onboard, however, and that gave Verville something of a fix, so he could call that in to Gloucester and they would tell him roughly where the cutter was. Verville would then discuss the information with Skipper Snyder and they'd agree on a heading, trying to keep on course for Gloucester but staying off the rocks near Baker's Island.

Vern DePietro remembers Bob Donovan at the wheel. "Bob's arms looked like he had been in a car wreck, they were so bruised. I also remember his feet coming out from under him a couple times and him sliding all the way over to the bulkhead of the wheelhouse. That's how steep the rolls were. Worst of all, we couldn't see the waves coming, just feel them. But we could see the snow swirling around because it was illuminated by the running lights. Red snow on the port side, green snow on the starboard side, and above it was white from the mast light. I didn't look at the snow for more than a couple seconds, as it would make me dizzy, and I was feeling crappy enough."

Seasickness was a problem for most of the *Cape George* crew. Seaman Dennis Hoffer did not normally get seasick, but that night was different: "I was on my knees puking out the starboard side door. Myron came over, and he was sick, too. He was standing above me, and his puke and the sea foam covered me. It wasn't much better for the newer guys down below, but even that was dangerous when the TV ripped away from the wall and went flying by them."

Hoffer sums up those tense minutes this way: "I really thought we were all going to die. I went below once, and I stopped in the mess deck where a prayer for mariners was posted on the wall. I'd looked at that prayer a hundred times before and it never meant anything to me, but that night it sure did, and I said every line. A few years later, in October of 1991, I was on a rescue attempt during the Perfect Storm. Even that storm wasn't as bad as the blizzard. The blizzard was absolutely terrifying."

SILENCE

When Paradis lost communication with the *Can Do*, he feared the worst, because he reasoned that if the boat was still afloat, Charlie would have transmitted on one of the portable radios. Yet the station commander held out hope. He encouraged the crew of his embattled forty-one-footer to stay just beyond the Eastern Point breakwater and keep searching.

At approximately one thirty A.M., the coxswain of the Forty-One radioed Paradis that they were one hundred yards off the breakwater. They had adjusted their radar for two miles but still had no contact with the *Can Do*. Paradis could hear the trepidation in the young coxswain's voice and knew he was taking a calculated risk keeping the small utility boat exposed to the furious seas. In a night of calculated risks—some wise and some not—Paradis was not ready to call in his Forty-One, and he radioed the crew with further instructions.

"Maintain position off the breakwater and around Rock Shoal if you can, and keep yourself heading in if possible and remain in that area and keep scanning."

"Roger. I'm not sure how long we can hang on out here; it's really roaring."

"I understand. We have people in jeopardy."

"I understand, too. Over."

Paradis then tried once again to raise Charlie or Frank: *"Pilot boat* Can Do, *pilot boat* Can Do, *this is Gloucester Station, channel twelve, over."*

Paradis waited for a reply, but heard only the crackling static of empty airwaves. He tried again, and still no answer. He called Warren Andrews, thinking maybe his location in Salem might yield better results: *"Warren, I'm concerned; how about trying to raise Frank on sixteen and twelve?"*

Warren gave it a shot: *"Pilot boat* Can Do, *pilot boat* Can Do, *Salem Control, Salem Control. Sixteen FM. Answer up, Frank."*

Warren was almost pleading, as if through the sheer force of his will he could make Frank get on the air.

Next, Coast Guard Group Boston tried: *"Pilot boat* Can Do, *pilot boat* Can Do, *this is Coast Guard Boston; can you read?"* There was no reply.

Paradis continued trying to make contact, then stopped to check on the Forty-One: *"How are you maintaining yourself out there?"*

"Be advised, Mr. Paradis, it's getting worse out here; I cannot maintain a position close to the breakwater; every time I come up around, I get blown over into Norman's Woe. I'm slowly coming back into the harbor. Making headway just a little bit."

In a defeated tone, Mike Paradis answered, *"Roger. Keep an eye out for* Can Do.*"*

"Roger. At this time my port engine is just about ineffective."

The modern technology of radios, radar, and high-performance engines was no match for the storm. As the Forty-One limped back into the harbor, the men of Coast Guard Station Gloucester held out little hope for the *Can Do.*

~

Coast Guard Group Boston, located on Atlantic Avenue at the foot of Hanover Street in Boston, is the operations coordination center for individual stations from Scituate, Massachusetts, north to the New Hampshire line. Paradis asked Group Boston to assist in trying to make contact with the *Can Do* because Group Boston's radio was tied into a number of antennae strategically placed at high points along the coast.

Suddenly, about 1:45 A.M. the radio operator at Group Boston heard a very weak transmission as if from another planet: *"Be advised we just took a big one over the bow and lost our windshields. Frank's hurt. Do you have any boats in our destination?"*

The *Can Do* was still afloat! The voice, however, did not sound like Charlie's or Frank's and might have been that of Donald Wilkinson, talking on the handheld marine VHF radio operated by portable batteries. The main radios had been rendered useless when water coming in through the windshield opening covered the vessel's electrical system and shorted them out.

Group Boston responded to the *Can Do* that the *Cape George* was having a hard time and the *Decisive* was on its way.

Then seconds later, another stunning surprise: *"Busted out the windshield. I thought we hit bottom, but maybe we took a bad sea. I'm not quite sure. Pretty shallow. Trying to take it easy here now. No idea at the present time of our location."*

The person talking was Frank Quirk. Remarkably, the tone of Frank's voice was no different than before the Mayday. It was calm, collected, and thoughtful, trying to give what little information he could to would-be rescuers. The stoicism—rather than alarm—expressed by Frank was his natural response to a crisis, but it was also meant to hearten his crew. And judging from the rest of the crew's handling of the Mayday situation, all the men were showing a spirit worthy of the boat's name. They were simply doing their best despite the pressure and odds stacked against them. They were not ready to think of the *Can Do* as their casket.

The fact that the *Can Do* was still afloat after a six-hour battle was a testament to the skills of the crew. The enormous waves, now thirty feet and greater, were still the biggest hazards the pilot boat faced, particularly climbing the breaking waves without any visibility beyond the mattress-stuffed windshield. If a vessel starts to climb a wave but cannot make the crest, it will slide back down, burying the stern. Then the same wave will push the bow up and over and the pilot boat will pitchpole to its doom.

For the crew of the *Can Do*, the goal of finding the mouth of Gloucester Harbor had been replaced by simply trying to keep the boat afloat.

After receiving the transmissions from the *Can Do*, Group Boston immediately contacted Warren Andrews and Mike Paradis with the news, *"Were you aware that I just had contact with the* Can Do*? We're picking them up on our remote speakers, believe it or not."*

Warren and Paradis were ecstatic. Just minutes earlier, they were beginning to think the worst, and now they learned that not only was the *Can Do* afloat but also Frank was on his feet. Warren was likely thinking, *Hang on a little longer, guys. This storm has got to ease up soon.* It was a realistic thought, based on prior storms' durations, like that of the one that split the *Chester Poling* in two. But the blizzard and its assault on the Northeast were beyond the realm of Warren's experience, just as they were for most everyone who lived through the events.

A second later, Group Boston told Warren, *"I'm going to make another call to them in five minutes. Were you able to get bearings on them earlier?"*

"I took an RDF on the Can Do *just before they lost their main radios, and I got a good reading, although very heavy snow static, of one hundred degrees from this station."* RDF is short for radio direction finder. It gave Warren the direction from his base to the *Can Do*. But to get a meaningful location for the *Can Do*, another

RDF would need to be taken from a different radio position, and where the two lines crossed would yield a fairly good estimate.

"Roger. Was that one hundred degrees from Salem Harbor, is that correct?"

"Roger. That is right; that is from Salem Control. In your last contact I was not able to read the Can Do. *Do I understand someone was injured?"*

"Roger. We believe it was Frank. They patched him up, and he will probably need stitches, and they are holding their own. They gave us a rough estimate of their position: three miles north of the breakwater, three miles south of the breakwater, or three to five miles out from the breakwater."

"Has the cutter Cape George *had any sightings on her radar regarding the* Can Do*?"*

"They were having a rough time also. If you don't have anything further, I'm going to go back to sixteen and make a call to the Can Do *in a couple minutes."*

The *Cape George* was having more than a rough time—the crew was literally fighting for survival, just like the crew of the Forty-One. Bill Cavanaugh remembers that even when the Forty-One was in shouting distance of Station Gloucester, they were still in danger. They couldn't tie up at the station because they thought they'd be swept into the parking lot, so they went to a more protected pier by the Empire Fish Company. As they tied up at the concrete pier, Cavanaugh remembers being awed by the way water was coming through openings in the pier like geysers.

The *Decisive*, at 210 feet, was a bit safer than the other two

Coast Guard vessels but was in a battle of its own, three to five miles south of Salem Sound. Rich Fitcher, a machinery technician, spent much of the night down in the engine room. "I was really concerned about how much icing was occurring up top, because we took some incredible rolls. No one on board had ever experienced anything like it, particularly being so close to land. The wind would occasionally come in from a different angle, and it must have been a nightmare for the helmsman whenever the wind and seas weren't aligned. It was challenging just to keep on course. I spent thirty years in the Coast Guard, including time in the North Atlantic, and I never encountered seas that could even compare to that night."

Fitcher was in the engine room with Jim Sawyer, an engineer. "When you feel the whole boat shudder," says Sawyer, "and literally moan, you can't help but be concerned." Fitcher was able to get up to the bridge, but things were no better. "The bridge is about midship, and when I was there, I remember looking dead ahead and seeing a wall of water at eye level. That's forty-eight feet. I know the height because there was a little placard in the bridge along a line that said 'forty-eight feet above the surface.' I have no idea how the smaller cutter and boats managed. The *Cape George* would have looked like a tiny cork out there."

Rich Fitcher recalls there were three civilians on board the *Decisive*. They were supposed to have been dropped off at Boston, but because of the emergency, they had to stay on the cutter. One of them was a fisheries inspector, and of all the people who were sick, he was the worst. The corpsman gave him shots of tranquilizers, and this man spent the night of the blizzard alternating between vomiting and unconsciousness. There were also two sea cadets on board. These were two fourteen- or fifteen-year-olds who were supposed to be on board just briefly for the experience to complement what they were learning in their classes. "They were terrified," said Fitcher, "but then again, we were pretty scared ourselves."

When Group Boston tried again to make contact with the *Can Do,* the strength of the vessel's radio signal had weakened further.

"This is Group Boston; say everything again; say everything twice. Over."

There was a faint, unintelligible response from the pilot boat. Group Boston desperately tried to maintain contact. Over and over, Group Boston said, *"Pilot boat* Can Do, *pilot boat* Can Do, *Coast Guard Boston Group, Coast Guard Boston Group, over."*

Group Boston heard an inaudible response and shouted back, *"Pilot boat* Can Do, *this is Group Boston. I believe I hear you very, very broken; say everything twice."*

Frank could barely be heard: *"Taking a beating. I'm trying to build up some power. I'll call you back in about five minutes."*

Frank did not call back in five minutes, and neither Group Boston, Warren Andrews, nor Mike Paradis at Station Gloucester was able to reestablish contact. It seemed the *Can Do,* alone in the impenetrable darkness, had finally lost its only connection to the rest of the world as a result of the weakening batteries in the handheld radio. On the pilot boat, it must have been devastating to the men's morale to hear Warren and the Coast Guard calling to them over and over and know that their replies could not be heard. Whatever their fates, they were once again alone in the black void of the tempest. What they didn't know was that high on a hill in the seaside town of Beverly, their words were being picked up loud and clear.

A tall, thin, bespectacled amateur radio operator named Mel Cole had been listening in on the plight of the *Can Do* for the last several hours. The fifty-three-year-old engineer and business-man was seated before his radio apparatus in the finished base-ment of his modest house.

Cole's house sat high atop Indian Hill in Beverly, just a half mile from the northern shore of Salem Sound. Mounted on the roof was a forty-five-foot rotating antenna capable of receiving and transmitting messages to ham radio operators around the world. The antenna was surrounded by enormous white pines and hemlocks that protected it from the full force of the wind, probably the only reason it was still standing.

Mel's equipment was a bit more sophisticated and exten-sive than that of the typical ham radio operator because of his knowledge of electronics. He had designed and invented several pieces of electronic equipment, and that background had spilled over to his radio transmitters and receivers. In fact, he had so much radio equipment in his basement, where he could sit in a chair on wheels and scoot from one communication device to another, that he called the office the radio shack. In front of him, arranged along a wall-length desk and cabinets, were a marine radio, a two-meter radio, two low-band radios, and tape recording devices connected to the communication equipment. He had his own little "mission control," and that night it proved to be invaluable, as he and his equipment were the only link with the *Can Do*.

Mel had learned about the *Can Do*'s mission to Salem Sound earlier that night from Warren Andrews. "Warren and I were good friends," says Cole, "because we were both radio operators, and we would get together from time to time. Through Warren, I also met Frank. It seemed like whenever Frank was in Salem and he had a free minute, he would walk over to Warren's place and say hello. I'd be visiting Warren, and Frank would pop in, and I got to know him. In fact, it seemed most everyone in the area knew Frank—he was like the hub of the waterfront group. He cast a wide net of acquaintances, and people always enjoyed his company. He had that rare quality of being laid-back and easy-going but was extremely bright. I quickly realized Frank was a true ocean expert in a modest sort of way."

When the *Can Do* first set out for Salem, Mel's phone rang. It was Warren and he said, "Frank and the boys have just left Gloucester and are heading down to Salem." Warren then explained to Mel that the crew of the *Can Do* was going to help the Forty-Four that was in trouble. Mel recalls that Warren mentioned how the crew on the Coast Guard boat were all young and Frank was really concerned.

"I figured," says Mel, "if anyone could get to Salem Sound that night, it was Frank."

At 1:50 A.M., Mel realized he was apparently the only radio operator still able to hear Frank. He asked the Coast Guard for permission to intercede and communicate with the *Can Do*. Group Boston approved, while instructing Mel to pass along what he learned. "I broke in and told Frank I could read him. Mr. Paradis and Coast Guard Group Boston could only hear my voice, so I often repeated what Frank said. Warren was on the two-meter radio, and that way we could communicate without disrupting anything Frank said. Then on the phone I had Jim Loew at the rescue center, so he could give advice. I was basically the go-between, passing communication back and forth. I also made a tape of all my conversations."

Frank heard Mel clearly and gave him an update: *"We have been aground, but we're off now. Still under our own power."*

Mel decided he had better get information on warding off hypothermia, and while he was making this request of Jim Loew, a voice from the *Can Do*—not Quirk's—shouted on the airways, *"We've lost it! It's all gone! We've had it!"*

"Beverly Base to Can Do, *Beverly Base to* Can Do, *come in. Beverly Base to* Can Do, *Beverly Base to* Can Do, *come in."*

Mel repeatedly called, but no one answered. The time was 1:55 A.M.

THE ANCHOR

Around two A.M. Mel was taken from the depths of helplessness and despair to a mood of guarded euphoria and relief. Mike Paradis radioed Mel and said, *"We have had an unconfirmed report that all of the* Can Do *crew have been rescued and have been taken to a hospital in Manchester."*

Mel allowed himself to relax and responded, *"Roger—that's mighty good news."*

Paradis used the word *unconfirmed* because the report had come in from an unidentified CB operator with few details other than to say all the men were alive and at the hospital. Nevertheless, Mel felt jubilant. "I was so tired and grateful," he recalled, "that I didn't stop to think there isn't any hospital in Manchester."

Mel was brought back to reality when he heard a weak, static-filled voice from the radio. It was Frank: *"Tell them it isn't true."*

Apparently Frank had heard the radio chatter about his alleged rescue. He then went on to describe his latest battle: *"Hard aground. No power. Taking on water."*

Throughout the night Frank, Charlie, and the crew had somehow managed to get the boat off the shoals each time they entered shallow water. But now three of the very worst things that can happen to a boat had befallen the *Can Do*—and all occurred simultaneously.

The pilot boat ran aground on one of the many rock ledges that litter the ocean off Salem. There is a particularly bad section of water just south of Baker's Island. It is a labyrinth of ledges, many lying just two or three feet below the ocean's surface. This region, which covers about a square mile, is known as the Gooseberries, named after the two tiny islands, North and South Gooseberry, that rise up from the uneven ocean floor.

Of all the locations where the *Can Do* possibly went aground, this was the most likely. Although Frank earlier believed he was somewhere outside Gloucester Harbor, the wind and waves were so strong that even though he was under power trying to head north, the seas were actually pushing the boat slowly backward, to the south. Over the course of the night, the *Can Do* likely slipped just to the east of Baker's Island and then into the treacherous waters of the Gooseberries. This location was close to where Warren Andrews made his radio fix on the pilot boat and was consistent with where both Mel Cole and another radio operator, Robert Wood, estimated Frank's position to be. Ironically, the *Cape George* and the *Can Do* likely passed within a half mile of each other, but without radar, neither could locate the other.

Frank knew the Gooseberries as if they were his own backyard, and he had enjoyed many happy times there. Often when he was out with his family for a Sunday boat ride, he would drop anchor at North Gooseberry Island. The kids would swim and dive for lobsters, and later the family might picnic on the island.

In the early morning of February 7, 1978, all Frank would have needed was just a speck of light, even the glow of a quarter moon, and he could have steered clear of these shoals. Instead he might as well have been blindfolded, with no radar, no lights, not even a windshield to look through. It was as if the storm had conspired with the night and together they had set a trap at the Gooseberries. The blizzard had been hunting various prey— the *Can Do*, the *Cape George*, and the *Decisive*—and now it had settled on cornering the smallest boat. The enormous waves had finally succeeded in stopping the *Can Do* and killing its main engine, probably by totally engulfing the boat and sending water down the exhaust stack.

Earlier the men on the Forty-Four related how the hum of the engine gave them a certain degree of comfort, and for the men on the *Can Do,* it must have been the same. Now, with the engine dead, the full roar of the storm was the only sound they could hear, except perhaps the sickening grinding of the hull on the rocks below. It's little wonder one of the men said, "It's all gone! We've had it!"

Whoever uttered that desperate cry knew that without power, the seas would eventually lift the boat off the rocks. Then the next big wave would probably catch it broadside, driving it over until it capsized. No matter how calmly Frank radioed their latest predicament, they all knew their situation had gone from critical to almost hopeless. The crew was reaching the limits of their endurance. They had been physically battered from the ceaseless pounding of the waves, and no doubt some or all of them had been weakened by seasickness. Winter's icy fingers were further adding to their discomfort, making them shiver uncontrollably, adding to their exhaustion. Death, it seemed, was just outside the aluminum walls of the pilothouse, and it now had the upper hand.

The men knew that it would be an incredible long shot for the *Cape George* or the *Decisive* to find them at night. Their only realistic hope of survival would be if the storm either abated or moved offshore. Then they could hang on until daylight and shoot up the case of flares that was stowed on the boat. But the storm was still stalled south of Nantucket Island.

Not only was the storm spinning in place, but also its dry center, called the occlusion, actually wobbled, making a small loop. The blizzard was like an angry bull trying to bust out of his corral, whose rage only intensified because he was unsuccessful. With nowhere to go, the storm spewed out its wrath to the north, concentrating its most destructive force directly at the region where the *Can Do* was foundering.

~

At 2:15 A.M. Frank came back on the radio: *"We've got an anchor set and are holding our own. Taking a beating but no further injuries. Trying to build up some power and get things started again. Our position unknown."*

Mel answered, *"Okay, Frank, we copied that. We understand you are anchored and everyone is all right and things are essentially unchanged. You're getting beat up where you are, but you are apparently in no immediate danger. I presume Coast Guard Boston and Gloucester have copied that. I'll be standing by, Frank."*

Dropping anchor was one of the last options available to the crew, but how had they done it? The anchor was located on the outside deck of the bow. It could only be dropped if someone actually went outside and unlocked the release mechanism. This would take incredible courage, because the chances of being swept overboard were greater than those of making it back inside. The same scenario had played out earlier on the Forty-Four when Paradis told McIlvride to *drop your hook*. McIlvride gave Paradis lip service, saying *roger*, but he had no intention of doing so—at least not until it was absolutely necessary. His crew felt the same way. They knew that just one ill-timed wave could come over the bow and pluck them off the way a shark would snatch a wounded seal.

Unfortunately, the crew on the *Can Do* could not restart their engines as the men on the Forty-Four did and had little choice but to get an anchor set. The waves probably swept the *Can Do* off the ledge, leaving it wallowing in the sea, where it would be only a matter of time before it capsized. Without engine power, there would be no way for Frank to keep the vessel's bow pointed into the waves, unless, of course, the anchor was set. An anchored boat will swing to the wind with bow headed into the seas, thereby avoiding a broadside wave while reducing the surface area hit by the wind. The boat will still have plenty of violent motion, because a vessel with a single anchor set will "horse" on its anchor chain, moving in a figure-eight.

It's unknown who set the anchor, but the decision to do so must have been made within seconds of either the grounding or being swept free. The anchor-dropping person would not have been Frank, because he was injured. Among the remaining men, Curly, Fuller, Wilkinson, or Charlie Bucko, the most likely one was Charlie.

Pete Lafontaine, Charlie's commanding officer at Point Allerton, believes the logical choice would have been the former Coastie. "Charlie," says Pete, "was trained specifically in heavy weather seamanship, and that included dropping the anchor." Frank III, who had performed the chore hundreds of times on the *Can Do*, concurs: "Charlie had been out in the soup before, and he was the youngest of the men on board. I've thought long and hard about who dropped that anchor, and it's almost miraculous that they were able to do so in those conditions."

The *Can Do* had two anchors, and both were on the bow. On a night like the blizzard, the big picket anchor, weighing seventy-five to one hundred pounds, would have been used. The anchor was fastened to ten feet of chain for extra strength when it was down among the rocks. Attached to the chain was an eyehook followed by two hundred feet of inch-and-a-half-thick nylon line, an excellent material for the purpose because of its elasticity and ability to minimize shock.

Before Charlie went out on the open deck, a safety line would have been fastened around his waist, although its usefulness was doubtful should he end up in the churning seas. His crew might have been able to haul him back toward the boat, but twenty-foot waves would have smashed him against the hull long before the crew could have pulled the 210-pound Charlie up to the gunnel. Charlie also may have donned a wet suit, which would give him a few extra minutes of life if he went in the water. Equally important, the rubberized wet suit would have provided better traction for crawling on the ice-covered deck.

Imagine the anxiety and tension during each of Charlie's moves to get to the anchor. When he was ready to go, the crew members would have opened the pilothouse door and the shrieking wind and stinging snow would have felt like birdshot peppering Charlie's face. Crawling on his belly, he'd have to keep one hand on the stanchions as he inched forward, timing his movements between waves as the *Can Do* reared and plunged. Spray would slash at his exposed flesh, and the howling wind would take his breath away. One misplaced knee or hand would send him sprawling and sliding, and the next wave easily could take him before he could recover. Ice breaking off the bow, from either Charlie's weight or the crashing of the boat, would fly like shrapnel, just as the bomb fragments had when he was wounded in Vietnam. Each time a wave came down on the bow, Charlie would be covered by hundreds of pounds of pure fury, trying to break his hold.

Once he reached the bow, where the anchor lay, the most difficult part of the maneuver would begin. In the dark, with frozen fingers, he'd unlock the anchor release. Then he'd need to break the hundred-pound anchor free of the ice and somehow lift it over the gunnel and steel railing that encircled the boat. Finally, after he let out the proper length of chain and line, he'd have to tie the line to the electric winch. This would be akin to tying your shoes while riding on the back of a rodeo bull.

As difficult as dropping the anchor was, somehow they got it done, and it bought them more time. Now the anchor chain and line had to hold.

~

Back on Indian Hill in Beverly, Mel told Frank he was still trying to get a fix on his location.

Frank in turn gave Mel a quick update: *"No luck on the power. Thirty-two-volt batteries all shorted out. Can't get the engine started. I have a mattress stuffed in the window to keep the seas out, and the boys have me pretty well patched up. Water not building up in the boat at this time."*

"Okay, Frank, I copy. Stand by. On your last transmission there was so much snow static that we could not get a cross bearing on you. Sorry we can't pin you closer. I am telling the story just as you give it to me—sorry we can't do more for you but am conveying your info just as you tell it."

Commander Paradis was listening, but since he could only hear Mel, he was anxious to learn exactly what was going on.

Paradis told Mel, *"Pass along whatever information you have on them."*

"Roger. The anchor is still holding. They have a mattress in the front window, and they're keeping the seas out pretty well. The water is not building up on them intolerably. They are having no luck at all in getting their batteries up and getting their engines on. The thirty-two-volt battery is shorted out. They can't seem to get it back on, so they can't start their engines. They are taking a beating from the seas. But they are in no worse shape, generally speaking. No one's been injured any more than before. Go ahead."

"Roger—appreciate your information. Ah, the next time you are in contact with them, try and make an effort to see who has been injured. We're getting an awful lot of phone calls. And also Frank's wife is involved here."

"Sorry we didn't convey that to you; it's Frank that has been injured."

"Serious or not so serious?"

"He says it's cuts and that's about it. I'm assuming he's doing much of the work there, so that it is not serious. He's been cut up with flying glass, and he's apparently doing all right; he's doing most of the talking."

Mel's comment about the *Can Do*'s dead thirty-two-volt battery didn't mention the boat's second battery. It was a smaller twelve-volt battery that powered the boat's lights, the heads, and, most important, the bilge pumps. Earlier Frank mentioned he was "trying to raise some power," which implied all power sources were dead. With inoperable bilge pumps, water would slowly accumulate at the base of the hull, and as each new wave slammed the bow, the water inside the boat would slosh around, adding to the instability. There was nothing more, however, the men could do to secure the vessel. Now it was a matter of waiting out the storm and hoping the wounded boat would stay afloat. The men had played their last card when they dropped the anchor, and their fate was out of their hands.

THE BREAKWATER

The crew on the *Cape George* feared running aground as they navigated north past the shoal waters around Baker's Island and toward the breakwater (protective jetty made of stone) at Gloucester. No matter how thick the steel on the cutter's hull was, it would be no match if thirty-foot waves pounded the boat into granite. And if the men on board needed a reminder of the cutter's vulnerability, they only had to think back on what had started this awful night: the failure of the hull on the giant *Global Hope*.

All night long Glen Snyder and Myron Verville had successfully kept the *Cape George* in deep water and away from land. But now they estimated they were near the entrance to Gloucester Harbor. Finding the opening without navigational aids would be extremely difficult, with no room for error. On the plus side, the harbor mouth opens to the south. With a little luck, they might be able to grope their way toward the opening and not have to make any dangerous turns. But they still had to contend with the breakwater. It extends across a third of the entrance, providing one last treacherous obstacle before safety.

Dennis Hoffer says this was the part of the voyage that he will never forget: "Myron had relieved Glen for a few minutes so he could go below. I was on the bridge with Myron and Bob Donovan, trying to find the harbor entrance, but the buoy [marking the entrance] had been dragged away by the waves. Glen was just climbing the ladder back to the bridge when he shouted, 'Turn! Turn!' I just had time to look out the starboard window, and all I saw was an enormous wall of white water. I didn't even have time to shout. The wave hit us, and the whole boat seemed to fly and shudder at the same time. Glen shouted, 'What did we hit?' I hollered back, 'It was a wave!' I later learned Glen thought he saw the breakwater directly ahead of us when he shouted, 'Turn.'"

Myron says the wave picked up the ninety-five-foot cutter and tossed them airborne at least the length of the boat. When the commanding officer shouted, "What did we hit?" Myron shouted back, "Nothing," but Snyder couldn't believe the seas could toss a boat as big and as heavy as the *Cape George* that far. To this day, Myron remains convinced that had they made that tight turn in the open sea and not at the harbor entrance, they would have rolled.

Although Dennis, Myron, and Bob Donovan believe it was a wave near the breakwater that made the boat shudder, others on board, such as crewman Gene Shaw, think they actually hit the breakwater before being hurled over it. Gene was down below, closest to the hull: "When we were somewhere close to the breakwater, I went down to the engine room to see what help I could give Mike Leonard. Mike was the engineer, and he had been down there all alone in that tiny engine control room. Suddenly this mountainous wave picked us up, then slammed us down so hard all four engines died. Mike and I immediately hit the compression release and starter button on each engine to get them back going. I think that big wave had lifted our propellers out of the water and the force of the fall was so hard the engines died. A couple seconds later, I heard a loud bang, unlike any of the noises the boat had made from the waves. Then we were suddenly in calm water. We had gone over the twenty-five-foot breakwater, and a section of the hull actually hit it."

Whatever actually happened to the *Cape George* in those terrifying seconds, the outcome was that the cutter was now inside the confines of the harbor and was safe.

~

While we know what the men on the *Cape George* were thinking and feeling, we can only speculate about some of the thoughts and actions of the *Can Do*'s crew. First and foremost, they were trying to keep warm, because without power, the *Can Do* had been transformed into a steel freezer. The men would have gone through all the clothes drawers in the captain's and mates' quarters and replaced their wet clothing with as much dry clothing as they could layer on. This was no easy task in the battering seas and would have certainly added more bumps and bruises to the ones they already had sustained.

Most of the time the men were wedged in a sitting position around the table aft of the pilothouse, using their hands and arms to keep their bodies from sliding and banging. They already had put on their life jackets, but they knew that if they did end up in the ocean, the life jackets really didn't matter; they'd be dead from exposure in ten minutes. The real reason they put on life jackets was because they thought of their families—their bodies had a better chance of being recovered if they floated. They knew that as much as their families would suffer if they were found washed up onshore, the pain would be even worse if they were never found at all. Cold, somber thoughts, to be sure, but the men's minds were free to roam because there were no other tasks that could be done now that the anchor was set.

The lights were out, so the crew could only see by the bouncing glow of their flashlights. By now they were well beyond exhaustion and almost in a frozen, trancelike state. Yet sleep was impossible in such rampaging seas. They needed to continuously use their cramped muscles to brace themselves for each fall of the boat after a wave rolled below.

Time slowed to a surreal, painstaking crawl. Their lives were now split in two: life before the blizzard and life during the blizzard, with the last six hours making all their prior years almost an insignificant flash. Time was now measured in minutes that felt like drawn-out hours. Get through the next minute, that was the goal. If they allowed themselves to think of dawn, maybe, just maybe, this hurricane of snow would lessen to a point where the Coast Guard could launch a helicopter. If the winds were rocking the helo and the pilot couldn't safely lower the rescue basket to the *Can Do*, maybe the men on the boat could jump into the water and the rescue basket would scoop them up the same way Brian Wallace did in his helo during the *Chester Poling* rescue. It was a long shot, but it seemed like the only way they would escape their prison of water and ice.

Of all the deprivations they were suffering, it's doubtful any approached the agony of simply waiting. But what were they waiting for? Most of the potential outcomes were not something to dwell upon. The waiting experience must have been akin to what a critically ill patient feels when awaiting a last-ditch, dangerous surgery.

For Frank, there was no more wrestling the helm, no more working the throttle, and no more straining to see and feel the next incoming wave. He was suffering the same excruciating inactivity the others had been dealing with the last six hours. It must have been an awful experience for a man who was a natural problem solver, a doer. Getting the job done and working through problems was so essential to his being it was no wonder he named his boat after the Seabee motto.

In every other hurdle life had thrown at Frank, he'd always been able to analyze the problem and then go to work. So many of Frank's friends, when describing him, said "there was nothing that Frank couldn't do." His brother liked to say, "If Frank can't do it, nobody can." He had always operated in a proactive way, and now he could only wait and react.

Frank's head was wrapped in blood-soaked bandages. He might have suffered a concussion from the spinning window motor striking his forehead, giving him a throbbing headache. He and Dave Curley, the electrician, had probably discussed various ideas on how to bring back the power. Frank and Charlie surely discussed the engine and the merits of whether or not to try to drop another anchor. Like Charlie, it wasn't in Frank's nature to go down without a fight, and he likely was still thinking things through as if in a chess match. Even though he was seemingly out of moves, he could still make mental preparations for steps he would take if they made it to morning.

Frank's mind may also have been churning about the events that put the men in this position, wondering what he could have done differently. He probably regretted letting the men other than Charlie come on board. As for himself, he knew that given the same situation of two boats in distress, he'd go so long as he had a fair chance of success. He knew Charlie would do the same. They were cut from the same cloth in terms of toughness, but very different in personalities: where Charlie was gregarious and at times boisterous, Frank was more reserved and understated. They seemed to balance each other, each feeding off the other's differences. Frank was Charlie's unspoken mentor, passing along his knowledge and sharing common experiences. They were close, not like father and son, nor like brothers, but as friends who had the same passion for the sea. Both had proven they could take the heat when the going got tough.

Although Charlie was the logical choice to accompany Frank on such a dangerous trip, Frank may have rued his decision to call him. The phone call to Charlie had been made just a few hours earlier, but it must have seemed like a lifetime ago, they had been through so much.

Frank also had a concern the other men didn't have, and that was the knowledge that his family was probably listening to the home marine radio and heard the Mayday and the news that the windshield had blown in on the captain. At least the family was safe. Audrey and Brian were in the warmth of the house, Maureen with her husband and new baby, and Frank III in far-off Okinawa, distinguishing himself in the marines.

Frank's voice was calm on the radio and surely was the same with his crew, not because he didn't feel the anxiety but rather because he'd learned to keep it in check and not let it paralyze his decision-making ability. He was able to carry on, and with each new calamity he still functioned and did the next right thing. Like the rest of us, he would have felt surges of fear that night, but with men like Frank, fear doesn't necessarily lead to panic or freezing in the headlights.

Frank and crew had survived thus far through a combination of exceptional seamanship, a sturdy vessel, and sheer grit. But now it seemed that in this life-and-death match of wits versus power, Mother Nature was a breath away from checkmate.

DESPERATION

In many respects, the predicament of the men on the *Can Do* has similarities to that of mountain climbers who get into trouble and watch their options fail. Expert mountaineers recognize the danger inherent in their sport, which is reflected in one of their mottos: *Getting to the top is optional; getting back is mandatory.* The saying emphasizes the need to stay flexible and alter your plans if conditions warrant, which was what Frank did when he made the decision to turn back when the radar went out.

Even before he set out, Frank acknowledged he'd take it one step at a time and wasn't married to the plan, telling Paradis, "We'll give it a look ... we might be right back." Climbers and boaters both know that weather can throw a curve, equipment can fail, and injuries can mean abandoning the objective and retreating to safety. Keeping your options open and not being blindly committed to reaching the goal no matter what are essential to those who venture away from civilization.

Now Frank was without options and without power. The boat was not only pitching up and down against the anchor chain but was also rolling, with the pilothouse port and starboard windows alternately hitting the sea. The waves were steep and coming one after the other, with just a short span between each wave in the shallow, confused seas. For the men on board, it felt like they were first going up a steep hill and then, when they reached the top, there was nothing on the other side and the *Can Do* just fell into the trough or the next wave. This made the conditions worse than being far out on the open ocean where the swells may have been larger, but the distance between each one was longer, allowing the boat to ride up one side and then slide down the other. With each passing hour, the freezing spray continued to coat the pilot boat's superstructure, adding to the extra weight from the water collecting in the hull.

Slowly, the *Can Do* was sinking.

~

About the only mechanical item still functioning on the *Can Do* was the handheld radio, but at two thirty A.M., Mel Cole had difficulty hearing Frank. Mel feared he was going to lose all communication with Frank unless they talked more sparingly.

"Save your batteries," said Mel, "because you are breaking up a little bit. There's a rig with a powerful light onshore, there's a truck moving in with it, and he's been stuck a couple times. But they're heading down to the general area that they believe you to be from the very crude bearings we've been able to take. So you might from time to time—if somebody can see aft, and I assume shore is aft—see if you can pick up that light, and that will give us some encouragement, Frank."

"These batteries won't hold for much longer. I'll contact you in thirty minutes."

"Roger, Frank, save your batteries, and I'll be here when you come back."

Warren Andrews was listening and also had been receiving updates from Mel. He wanted to make sure everyone involved understood his estimation of Frank's location: "Beverly Control, this is Salem Control. My last reading when they had their main radios up was one hundred degrees. Now readings are very difficult with all this heavy snow static, but I feel it was a good reading at that time. That would be roughly a line between me and Baker's Island."

Mel acknowledged Warren's estimation and then waited a few minutes for Frank to come back on. When he did, Mel gave him the latest update: "Can Do, this is Beverly Base. I have been advised a truck with an extremely powerful light aboard is headed for Magnolia— keep your eyes open for it—Warren suggests you consider digging the auxiliary battery leads from the back of your radio and hook up to a twelve-volt battery to gain more power."

"We'd never get to the battery. Action too much out here."

A couple of minutes later, Mel came back on the air and let Frank know that Robert Wood was still trying to get a radio fix on him from Singing Beach.

Frank responded, *"Okay, Mel. Getting pretty cold and weak here—guess the loss of blood caused it. Keep getting wet, too."*

"Frank, why don't you get out of the wheelhouse and go below? I know water is coming in that window. Huddle in with the others and try to warm up. You can't do any good up there in the wheelhouse, and if she does beach, you're better off down below with the others. Tuck your walkie-talkie radio beside you when you lie down, as your batteries are getting low. You were broken on the last transmission, and the warmth will revive them."

A minute later, Mel gave both Group Boston and Chief Paradis an update on his last transmissions with Frank: *"I just spoke to the Can Do and I advised them to keep together and keep warm. Frank said three of the boys are below in sleeping bags and two are with him, which leads me to think he's counting wrong. He's in the wheelhouse and getting wet as the water comes through the mattress he has stuffed in the window. He's beginning to feel the weakness from the loss of blood that he took earlier in the battle and so I've tried to encourage him to go below with the others. But his batteries were breaking out on him, so I don't know whether he agreed to do it or not. But he did sound receptive to going below with the others; he's really gaining nothing by staying in the wheelhouse."*

Frank's last message indicated his injury was more serious than first supposed by Mel and Paradis. The impact from the shattered glass and the spinning window motor to Frank's head must have caused a deep gash rather than surface cuts. For Frank to even mention his weakness was a clear signal he was hurting far more than he'd been letting on. The weakness he felt was probably a result of not only the loss of blood but also exhaustion and the insidious effects of hypothermia. And when Frank, in his usual understated way, said he was getting pretty cold, one can assume that he was really chilled to the bone.

Hypothermia occurs when the body's core temperature falls below normal, and Frank was clearly in the early stage of this silent killer. Although he probably changed into dry clothing just after the windshield was blown out, he continued to get wet and was likely shivering uncontrollably. The last hour had been especially tough because without power there was no heat in the *Can Do,* and Frank was doggedly standing at the wheel or sitting at the wheelhouse table in freezing temperatures.

The cold had not robbed him of his common sense. He was still making sound decisions and explaining them in a logical way, such as when he rationalized that there was way too much motion on the boat for him to rewire the radio to a twelve-volt battery. He surely knew that going below might provide a bit more warmth, but he'd been reluctant to leave the pilothouse because, as he was the ship's captain, he felt almost an instinctive need to be near the vessel's controls. But without power and at anchor, there was little he could do, and Mel's advice was sound.

~

At 2:45 A.M. Mel asked Frank if he wanted to try switching from the handheld VHF radio to the CB radio, thinking maybe that would transmit better: *"Frank, do you want to try your CB?"*

"Don't think we'll try to move. Really ripping out here. We're pretty well wedged between the table."

Frank had not taken Mel's advice to go below, because he was still at the table in the pilothouse with another crew member. Maybe Frank thought that if he was going to die on the *Can Do* he wanted to go down near the wheel and not trapped in a sleeping bag. The rolling and pitching of the boat were so severe Frank didn't think it was even worth the effort to try to get to the CB radio. He must have felt as if he were inside a miniature glass snow globe being shaken by a giant hand. For six straight hours, the seas had battered Frank and his crew, with the last hour at anchor being the worst. The *Can Do* was thrashing and pulling on the anchor line like a kite in a gale ready to bust loose.

With the *Cape George* docked in Gloucester, the only ship that could possibly come to the *Can Do*'s aid was the *Decisive*. At approximately two A.M. the cutter had likely passed the *Can Do*, but because the ship's radar was malfunctioning, it never located the floundering pilot boat. The *Decisive* then continued a mile north, then held position in deep water about a half mile off the northern part of Salem Sound, near Magnolia.

During Frank's last radio message, Mel could hear a deep weariness in Frank's voice, and Mel decided he had nothing more to say. He told Frank he'd be standing by for whenever Frank wanted to make the next transmission.

A full forty-five minutes passed before Frank came back on

the air at three thirty A.M.: *"We're getting pretty wet up here. Hatch is loose, and we're going to try to move aft."*

"Okay, Frank, take your time and try to locate some food. You could use the energy. Keep your bodies in contact for warmth and put all the cover over you possible. Don't use your radio unless necessary and keep it between you to warm up the batteries—don't lay on the mike button by accident. Frank, it's only about two hours until dawn, and latest weather promises abating seas. Gloucester Coast Guard will get a forty-four-footer underway to your position then."

"Okay, Mel. Will hold on. Sure wish we could raise some power. It's really hopping out here, but we're making it."

"Okay, Frank. Don't waste your batteries; you were breaking up on that last transmission. Get some rest, and I'll be here when you call back."

Mel was praying the men could hang on for another couple of hours. But the loose hatch was yet one more ominous sign that the waves were chipping away at the boat's structural integrity. Although he'd told Frank that the seas would be abating soon, Mel had made that up, believing Frank needed some encouraging news to help make it until dawn.

A half hour passed, and when no word came from the *Can Do*, Mel tried to raise Frank:

"Can Do—*Beverly Base.*" No answer.

"Can Do, *this is Beverly Base.*" Still no response.

Mel let another agonizing half hour pass and at four thirty A.M., he tried again:

"Can Do—*Beverly Base.*" No answer.

Five minutes later, a voice came on the radio, but it was Group Boston and not Frank: *"Beverly Base, this is Group Boston; are you still able to raise the Can Do?"*

"That's a negative—it has been over an hour since my last contact—will keep trying. He had been coming on every half hour, and it's been an hour at least now. I have called him on the half hour and maybe more frequently just to let him know we are here. I did encourage him to go below with the rest of the crew and get him out of the pilothouse, which was getting wet due to the window being gone. He may have done it and the walkie-talkie won't reach from below. This is my supposition at this time."

At six thirty A.M., a trace of dim gray light filtered through the driving snow. The men on board the *Decisive* hoped that with the slightly improved visibility they could conduct a more thorough search for the *Can Do*. The intensity of the blizzard, however, was just as bad as the previous night. With intermittent radar the 210-foot cutter made sweeps of the coastal area with no results. When it reached the outskirts of Salem Sound, the cutter still could not risk venturing inside and stayed out in deep water. No one knew if either the *Can Do* or the *Global Hope* was afloat.

~

Back at the Quirk house in Peabody, Brian was trying to convince his neighbor Don Lavato to try to drive to Station Gloucester. There was now a travel ban in effect for all of Massachusetts, but Lavato was a policeman and, after listening to Brian's pleas, decided to give it a shot. Lavato's car was a big, heavy Lincoln

Continental, which did an admirable job of driving through deserted snow-clogged streets.

"There were a few drifts in excess of six feet," recalls Lavato, "so all I could do was punch through them. We couldn't do this too fast, because there might be a car under a drift. I think all my years driving a police cruiser paid off that day, because somehow we made it to Gloucester; then the car died."

They walked the final half mile to the station, weaving their way around the rocks and debris hurled up on Rogers Street. Outside the station they saw Coasties placing sandbags around the building, hoping their efforts would prevent the next high tide from inundating the ground floor. Lavato and Brian entered the station, and Paradis sat them down and explained what was being done and how there was still no news on the fate of the *Can Do*. Lavato recalls that Brian was smart enough to know things looked bleak after so much time without communication.

It was now midmorning, and there had been no word from the *Can Do* for over six hours. The Coast Guard men at the station all knew Brian Quirk, and they took him to the mess hall and tried to get his mind off the *Can Do*. Brian, however, wanted to know what they thought had happened to his dad. Ralph Stevens, the young seaman who had been on the Forty-One when it tried to go to the aid of the *Global Hope*, remembers it was an awkward situation.

"Brian was a nice kid," recalls Ralph, "and most everyone knew him because he was always with his dad on the *Can Do*.

We tried to say encouraging words to Brian that morning. Guys would come up to him and say things like 'Maybe the *Can Do* is hard aground onshore or washed up on some beach and your dad's wondering when we are going to find him.' We came up with all sorts of possibilities of how we were going to find the guys alive, even though in our hearts we had pretty much lost hope."

PART III

THE SEARCH

A lthough Warren Andrews had been on the radio for approx-imately thirty-six straight hours, at noon on Tuesday, he was still helping coordinate the search for the *Can Do*. His last radio fix on the pilot boat placed it somewhere near Baker's Island. He stubbornly held to the belief that the boat might be either wrecked on the island's granite shore or still holding at anchor near the island.

Without aircraft to search the island, Warren contacted the Baker's Island lighthouse keeper, asking him to try to walk the perimeter of the island. The lighthouse keeper did so, with no sighting of the *Can Do*. A half hour later, Warren asked him to try again. The lighthouse keeper responded, *"Warren, in the next couple of minutes I'll get bundled up and take another look around. Negative sightings so far. I'll get back to you in an hour. I'll make another sweep of the east side of the island from the lighthouse to the southern end of the island."*

The *Decisive* also moved in closer to Baker's Island but still was not able to enter the sound. The cutter's skipper gave Group Boston an update: *"Be advised weather conditions are still atrocious."*

"Roger. We will pass that to the air station. What is your present position right now?"

"We have less than two hundred yards visibility in snow, and the wind is blowing fifty-five, gusting to sixty-five, and I've got to wait probably for this to clear a little bit to get in there. Will stay off the shore until the weather abates and then look for flare sightings and also conduct a shoreline radar search."

"Roger. The Can Do *should give off an excellent radar presentation, being it's an all-steel construction."*

"Roger—do you have a clue on the Gooseberries? Is it up around Magnolia?"

"It is the section just south of Baker's Island."

"Roger. We will conduct a radar search of that area and then if it stops snowing and blowing, we should have a good chance of seeing if there are flares along the beach at night, and we will keep the air station informed."

In the meantime, Boston RCC was feeding data into a new but very basic computer search program in hopes that it could narrow the search area for the *Can Do*. The pilot boat's last known position, along with wind speed and elapsed time, was entered in the computer. The computer indicated that an area south of Baker's Island would be the likely spot the *Can Do* would have been pushed to if it had broken away from its anchor. Because the computer program was rudimentary, the indicated area was quite large, and the men had to use their own judgment on where to focus, ultimately settling on a ten-mile stretch of water from Baker's Island to Nahant.

Although no helicopters were ordered out in such hazardous conditions, pilot Brian Wallace, who had rescued some of the men off the *Chester Poling*, wanted to give it a try. "I asked my three-man crew," says Wallace, "if they wanted to risk going up to look for the *Can Do*, and each one said yes. All we knew was that the pilot boat lost its engines during the night, and we figured it was a long shot anyone on board was still alive. But we decided to go, and we took off from Air Station Cape Cod. Our helicopter was an HH-3F, weighing twenty-two thousand pounds, and we had about three and a half hours of fuel. The wind was blowing sixty knots, and it was snowing like mad. We flew especially high at about fifteen hundred feet. We hadn't gone very far—somewhere near Provincetown—when the crew noticed ice was building up on the nose dome."

Wallace could barely see out the windshield because of the icing, and he had to make a tough decision. He weighed the risks and realized that the situation he was in was different from that of the *Chester Poling* rescue. With the *Poling*, he had known there were still people alive on the tanker, whereas now he doubted the men on the *Can Do* had survived the night: "If we had confirmation that someone on the pilot boat was alive, I probably would have risked it and pushed on. The only possible way we might have made it would be to have gotten rid of some of the ice by flying really low over the ocean so that the salt spray would hit the helicopter, and maybe some of the ice might have melted. But we knew if that didn't work, we would have gone down, and if we went down that would be that—we'd be dead; there would be zero chance of survival. So we turned back and made it to base safely."

About midafternoon, Warren called the *Decisive* to check on their progress:

"Have you had any luck contacting the pilot boat Can Do?*"*

"We are two and a half miles south of Gloucester, and we did a radar search just south of Kettle Island and Great Egg Rock with negative results. We will stand by in this area until the weather abates. We'll keep you advised. Would appreciate a call if you hear anything further. Visibility is two hundred yards and still heavy snow."

Warren, exhausted to the point of collapsing, must have wondered if it would ever stop snowing.

~

Finally, just after nightfall on Tuesday, the driving snow and blasting winds began to slacken. It was at this time a chilling discovery was made by the Marblehead harbormaster, John Wolfgram. A boat fender with the name *Can Do* written on it had washed up in Marblehead. Wolfgram relayed the news to Station Gloucester.

Paradis had sent young Brian Quirk upstairs to the rack to get some rest, but Don Lavato was with the chief when the news came in. Although it didn't conclusively prove that the *Can Do* had sunk, the boat fender was a dire sign. An hour later, another call came in, and this one said a foam life ring buoy with the words *Can Do* had also been found.

"At that time," recalls Lavato, "Brian had woken up and came downstairs. Paradis then sat him down and said, 'You know what I'm going to tell you, don't you?' "

Brian struggled to hold back the tears and said, "Yes." Paradis then explained that in all likelihood, finding the debris from the *Can Do* meant the boat had capsized and the men aboard were dead. Lavato says Brian handled the situation as well as could be expected. "And Paradis," says Lavato, "did his best also. He didn't pass this unpleasant task on to somebody else; he did it face-to-face."

Mike Paradis had gone thirty-six hours without sleeping and had spent the prior night making life-and-death decisions as the station commander. He had almost lost his own boat crew on the Forty-Four. Now he felt that the men aboard the *Can Do* were drowned. He had kept his stress and anxiety largely in check, and he still had more difficult decisions to make with regard to sending boats out to look for the *Can Do*.

Perhaps the only time commander Paradis let his emotions get the best of him was earlier that morning when he went to the Cape Ann Marina. There he located Gard Estes and Louis

Linquata, looked them in the eye, and said, "I did not order those men to go out." Paradis didn't wait for a response; he simply turned around and went back to the station. Both Gard and Louis were somewhat taken aback, because neither of them had blamed Paradis for anything that had transpired.

~

Tuesday was also an especially difficult day for Frank's daughter, Maureen, and his wife, Audrey. The police had given Maureen, her husband, and their baby daughter a ride to Audrey's house that morning, and they spent the day monitoring the marine radio and conversing with Chief Paradis. Local news media contacted the Quirks for updates, adding to their stress. The *Daily Peabody Times* had a front page article titled "Rescue Try Hurts City Man." The paper reported "a Gloucester Pilot Boat was in trouble off the North Shore this morning in mountainous seas and blizzard conditions." It went on to say that "Quirk was apparently injured when a wave rushed over the craft."

The *Gloucester Daily Times* was more pessimistic in their coverage, titling an article "*Can Do* Feared Lost" and reporting that "the Coast Guard held out faint hope late this morning for skipper Frank Quirk and crew." The story described how the *Can Do* battled thirty- to forty-foot seas and lost power somewhere off the Magnolia coast before disappearing.

Despite the bleak picture painted by the newspaper and the finding of the *Can Do*'s fender, Maureen Quirk held on to her faith that her father had found a way to survive. "We waited at the house all day Tuesday," says Maureen, "and it seemed like time had dragged to a crawl. It snowed hard all day, and there was still no word from the *Can Do*. Even when they found the fender and life ring, I didn't give up hope—I thought somehow Dad would be found alive."

THE *GLOBAL HOPE*

During the early evening of Tuesday, February 7, the *Decisive* was, at long last, able to enter Salem Sound. Their radar was back in business, and while they could not locate the *Can Do*, they did, however, spot something much larger. Approximately halfway into the sound at Coney Island Ledge sat the *Global Hope*, hard aground and still intact.

The *Decisive*'s searchlight illuminated the six-hundred-foot hulk of steel, and men could be seen waving frantically on the deck. But the seas were still heavy and the wind had plenty of punch left, gusting to sixty miles per hour. Since the men on the tanker were in no apparent danger, the skipper of the *Decisive* wisely decided not to try for an immediate evacuation. The

Global Hope's crew would be safer on their crippled ship rather than attempting to disembark on a rope ladder dangling above the *Decisive's* bobbing rescue boat.

An hour later, the first helicopter successfully launched from Air Station Cape Cod and went directly to the *Global Hope*. The winds buffeted the chopper about and the pilot struggled to keep the chopper hovering above the tanker while a crew member kept their searchlight on the ship. Then they lowered a microphone, and for the first time since the original call for help the previous day, the Coast Guard could communicate with the *Global Hope*.

The tanker's captain reported that the men were safe but cold and that the ship had lost all power when water flooded the engine room. The Coast Guard responded that they should sit tight, and in the morning conditions should be moderate enough for the *Decisive* to evacuate them with their rescue boat.

Next the helicopter pilot began searching for the *Can Do*, first combing the inner shoals of Salem Sound while he continually tried to raise the missing pilot boat on the radio:

"Pilot boat Can Do, *this is Coast Guard Rescue Copter one-four-seven-three. If you can read us, we will be searching the general area, and you should be able to see our lights. If you have any kind of flares, set them off. We will be searching in the area. If you can transmit, come up on sixteen."*

Warren radioed the helicopter: *"Coast Guard Copter one-four-seven-three, this is Salem Control; last evening the pilot boat advised me he was approaching Baker's Island when his radar was blown away. He* came about and he was heading back to Gloucester. The Can Do *was a fifty-foot steel hull with five men on board. They have a ten-man life raft and have portable marine radios."*

Warren's choice of words is telling—he uses the past tense to describe Frank's boat, saying, "The *Can Do* was a fifty-foot steel hull." He knew that with no word from the *Can Do* in over eighteen hours, the outlook was bleak. Still, he wasn't going to abandon his radio until he literally dropped from exhaustion.

The pilot let Warren know he agreed with the suggestion to focus on Baker's Island: *"All right, we'll start at Baker's and look every island over. We've got the searchlight on, and we'll look at everything east. You said he did have a portable, so I think what we'll do is monitor sixteen in case he can hear us or if he's very weak we can hear him overhead."*

While slowly flying over Baker's Island, the pilot felt a ray of hope when he spotted footprints in the snow and wondered if they could be from one of the shipwrecked men on the *Can Do*. He immediately contacted the *Decisive*, whose skipper in turn radioed Warren:

"This is the cutter Decisive, *our helo is over Baker's Island, and they request to know if anyone is living at Baker's Island at the present time."*

"This is Salem Control. There is a caretaker at Baker's Island; he can be contacted on sixteen FM."

"Salem Control, cutter Decisive. *Roger, nothing further. This is the* Decisive, *out."*

When the pilot received this information, he contacted the caretaker directly:

"*Baker's Island, this is the helicopter. Do you live in the light or where are you living?*"

"*Negative on the light. We're, ah, in the large building right near the base of the pier; we're up top, over.*"

"*Did we just go by you?*"

"*That is affirmative, almost came in my window.*"

"*Aha, I thought I saw somebody in the bathtub! Ha. We're just looking for anybody in the* Can Do *and thought you would know about all those footprints.*"

Despite the pilot's attempt to break the tension with humor, being airborne at night in sixty-mile-per-hour winds and lingering snow was no pleasure ride, especially when flying just a few feet above the island and ocean. The footprints seen by the pilot were from the lighthouse keeper.

As the chopper pulled away from the lighthouse, the keeper quickly asked if there was any word about the fate of the *Can Do*.

The pilot responded, "*Nah, nothing definite; there's some wreckage down by Nahant that could possibly be from the* Can Do."

While the helicopter pilot was searching the waters around Baker's and Great Misery Island, a second helicopter took off from Air Station Cape Cod. On board was Barry Chambers, the commander of the Atlantic Strike Team based out of Elizabeth City, North Carolina. Chambers was accompanied by three other members of his team. It was their mission to find out if oil was leaking from the *Global Hope* and, if so, to figure out a way to minimize the flow and damage.

Chambers and his men were veterans, having battled oil spills up and down the East Coast. He knew that the *Global Hope* was not in jeopardy of sinking or breaking apart, but no one knew the status of its cargo of oil.

Before taking off, the strike team had boarded the helicopter with a minimal amount of gear that included diving equipment, a pump, and radios. "When we took off, flying conditions were marginal," recalls Chambers, "and we were buffeted about by fifty- to seventy-knot winds, and snow was still falling. I knew we were going to be dropped to a tanker in trouble, but that's about all the information I could get in advance."

When Chambers reached the *Global Hope*, the pilot did his best to maintain position above the tanker's deck. Chambers donned a harness known as a "horse collar," which attached around his upper body and beneath his arms. The harness was then clipped onto a wire cable, and Chambers stepped out of the copter and into the black void, to be lowered down.

"I don't think any of the crew on the *Global Hope* even knew we were being dropped down," says Chambers. "Nobody met us, so I sent my guys to scout out the ship, and I made my way down to the officers' dining area, and that's where we found the whole crew. I was angry at these people that they had panicked, particularly the captain. The tanker was high and dry up on a shoal and in no danger of breaking up. I talked to the captain very briefly and didn't cover my disgust. He had cried wolf, and he was still saying his crew needed rescuing."

Using flashlights, Chambers and his men negotiated their way farther into the belly of the tanker and found the engine room flooded, with oil on the top of the seawater. They then checked various cargo tanks to see how much oil was in the hold and to determine if they were flooded: "We eyeballed the level of the liquid in the tank, and if it was the same as the outside ocean level, that gave us a good indication there was a problem—which there was." Then the men took soundings around the vessel to determine the depth of water around the ship and calculate the ship's angle.

Chambers was aware that the *Can Do* was missing and was quite upset because he had gotten to know Frank the prior year, while doing work on the *Chester Poling* wreck. His team's job had been to cut three-foot-wide strips off the stern section of the hull. These would be examined for clues as to why the hull broke.

"Frank would come out on the *Can Do* to where we were working," says Chambers, "and watch what we were doing. He was very interested in how we did our work and interested in what we were learning about the *Chester Poling*. We would shoot the shit, and sometimes at the end of the day have a drink at the Cape Ann Marina where I was staying. He was very personable and straightforward. Good company."

When the job on the *Chester Poling* was just about over, Chambers "borrowed" the ship's bell and brought it back to Elizabeth City Air Station, where he hung it up in the Chief's Club. The bell was a large one, about eighteen inches in diameter and twenty-four inches tall.

"The night I got dropped down to the *Global Hope*, I couldn't help blame the captain for whatever had happened to Frank. All the captain had to do when he was first taking on water was to collect soundings to determine his depth. He would have known he was sitting hard aground and his vessel wasn't going to sink. It wasn't like the tanker was out on the open ocean. The crew and officers didn't care; once I got on board they just wanted off. None of those guys had any attachment to the ship—it was as if they had checked out a rental car and now they were done with it."

DEVASTATION

Sunrise on Wednesday morning revealed an incredible landscape to residents of eastern New England. Gone were familiar landmarks, replaced by a scene of stark white. Just about every tree, bush, road, and home was enshrouded in snow. People could not get out their doors, because the storm doors, which opened outward, were firmly sealed shut by snow that reached waist-high. The lucky ones had young teenagers who could climb out a window, flounder toward the door, and then scoop away the snow around the doorway so that parents could then step outside. Others went into their garage and opened the garage door, only to discover that snow had drifted to the roof, sealing them inside.

Those who could do so began the multihour task of shoveling

a short path toward the street. People who had an eye for natural beauty would surely have been awestruck at the way the snow blanketed over the straight lines of man-made objects, replacing sharp edges with smooth white curves. Drifts, looking like cresting waves, turned flat lawns into miniature mountain ranges, and the old familiar neighborhoods were virtually unrecognizable.

This was the scene most people woke up to, except those who lived along the coast, where the landscape looked more like a war zone. It was as if the sea had gone mad and left its normal domain to assault anything in its rampaging path. Over the course of the last two days, the sea had claimed several portions of the shore by carrying off huge chunks of land. Not since the Great Hurricane of 1938 had the coast been altered to such an extent. Through a combination of sheer power in the relentless pounding of waves, coupled with the more subtle but equally devastating erosion that followed, the Atlantic had reshaped the coastline.

In Gloucester and Rockport, coastal roadways looked like the surface of the moon; massive sections of asphalt had been ripped away, and the remaining sections were under three feet of fist-size cobbles and boulders as large as beach balls. Here and there, a lobster boat lay on its side, blocking the few sections of street that were free of debris. On one street, crabs, starfish, and lobsters were mixed in with the rubble, snow, and seaweed.

Many homes were destroyed just to the south of Boston in Scituate, Marshfield, Hull, and Kingston. Some had their second stories blown off, while others had lost their first floor, only to have the upper stories come crashing down. Homes were pushed off their foundations and back into marshes, or were carried piecemeal into the sea. Many of the survivors who had lived in those homes had only seconds to escape before the seas came crashing into their living rooms. The United Press International reported that "Scituate's Shoreline Isn't There Anymore."

The storm's fury lashed out as far south as New York and New Jersey. On Wednesday, February 8, the United Press International released an article with the heading "Drifts Blocking NYC Canyons." The report went on to say that the worst snowstorm to hit New York City since 1947 had paralyzed the city, stranding thousands of motorists and causing ten deaths in the metropolitan area. New York and New Jersey each received about eighteen inches of snow and strong, damaging winds, but both states recovered rather quickly, and by Wednesday many of the main highways were open.

Massachusetts and Rhode Island, however, were a different story. With thirty to forty inches of snow, they remained crippled well into the weekend. Thousands of cars were abandoned on highways throughout both states, but Route 128, the beltway around greater Boston, was in the worst shape, with three thousand cars and five hundred trucks stranded.

The police, fire department, and National Guard had their hands full rescuing stranded motorists, but they also had the grim task of searching for the missing. One of the most heart-wrenching events of the blizzard involved the search for ten-year-old Peter Gosselin, who had gone out to shovel snow and never returned. Peter lived in the small town of Uxbridge, Massachusetts, in the south-central part of the state, and on Tuesday afternoon, he and his brother went out to shovel the walkway of their grandparents, who lived a short distance away. The boys then returned to their own neighborhood on Mary Jane Avenue but became separated while playing. When Peter's brother came home without him, the family first checked their immediate neighborhood and then expanded their hunt to the grandparents' street with no results. The family then called the police, who immediately launched a full-blown search.

The search continued for several days, but not a clue to Peter's disappearance was found. Approximately three weeks later, the local postman noticed a mitten in the snow of the Gosselins' yard, next to the front doorsteps where an eight-foot pile of snow had melted down to three feet. When he went to pick up the mitten, he saw a boot. The letter carrier rushed to the house next door and called the police. Police Chief John Emerick arrived at the Gosselins' home and quickly located the boy's body, almost on the bare ground under the snow pile. Peter's head was up against the side of the cement steps, and his legs were higher than his torso, leading police to believe that he had fallen from a bank of snow next to the house and struck his head. It was a heartbreaking discovery, perhaps made worse with Peter just a few feet from safety.

~

On the Wednesday morning after the blizzard, the waves began to subside off Gloucester. The *Cape George* and Station Gloucester's two forty-one-foot utility boats set out from Gloucester Harbor to look for the *Can Do*. The boats headed south toward Baker's Island. On board one of the forty-one-foot utility boats was Bill Cavanaugh, and he remembers riding the huge groundswells all the way down to Salem Sound: "I remember seeing the *Decisive* enter Salem Sound, and I was glad I wasn't on it. They were rolling at unbelievable angles. I'm sure the guys on the *Decisive* were looking back at us and thinking, *Thank God we're not in that little boat.*"

The other forty-one-footer was piloted by Bob McIlvride: "We were down near Marblehead, and the swells were still ten to fifteen feet, but our boat was handling well. There was no sign of the *Can Do*, and I kept thinking about what might have happened to them. I had heard about how the windshield crashed in on Frank, and my thought was that it was a log that did it rather than a huge wave. I thought about different scenarios of what might have happened after their last communication, but I wasn't optimistic we'd find anyone alive."

Inside Salem Sound, the *Decisive* moved closer to the *Global Hope*. Crew members from the cutter then lowered a twenty-foot motor surfboat to the ocean and made the short run to the tanker. *Global Hope* crew members immediately began climbing down a hanging ladder thrown over the side of the ship. The surfboat then ferried the men back to the cutter. *Decisive* crew member Rich Fitcher says that once the *Global Hope*'s crew came on board, they quickly got them down into the heated mess deck. "Only one man could speak English," says Fitcher, "so he was the translator and spokesman. I remember how cold those men were and how they stayed cold for a long time. I guess that big chunk of steel didn't exactly retain any warmth."

~

At the very time the crew of the *Global Hope* was being ferried to the warmth of the *Decisive,* the fate of the *Can Do* became known. Warren Andrews, worn out and haggard, was back on his radio, and a call came in from one of his friends at the Boston Yacht Club.

"Good morning, Warren. I just wondered if you got the message the Marblehead PD wanted you to call?"

"Ah, Boston Yacht Club, this is Salem Control, roger, roger. Thank you very much for that, sir. I'll get to them right away. It's just with all these receivers going and telephones I probably didn't hear his call."

Warren called the Marblehead police and heard the words he'd been dreading: Frank was dead. The sea had just given back his body.

The Marblehead police had received a call from the police officers in Nahant that a body, identified by a driver's license as Frank Quirk, had been found on Nahant's Short Beach, approximately eight nautical miles south of Baker's Island. Frank was dressed in street clothes, frozen stiff, and clinging to a life preserver. On his body was a service revolver, as Frank was a special on-call police officer. A second body, later identified as that of Don Wilkinson, was found just a hundred yards away. The police put both victims on two sleds and started pulling them toward the station. Frank's body fell off the sled and rolled like a snowball back toward the sea. The police officers retrieved it and resumed their sad trek. Once at the station, the bodies were held in the garage until a Coast Guard helicopter was sent to fly them back to Station Gloucester.

Ironically, Bob McIlvride had just returned to the station and assisted in taking the bodies off the helicopter. "That's when it all sank in," says McIlvride. "Prior to that, I probably took it for granted that when we went out on rescues, everything would work out. Maybe the *Chester Poling* had something to do with it. Even though I wasn't involved, I was at the station when that occurred, and I remember how pumped up everyone was about that rescue. We were all gung ho. That's why we joined, and the *Chester Poling* reinforced that we could go out in terrible conditions and handle them. But after carrying the body bags out of the helo, it hit me that there are other outcomes."

Seaman Ralph Stevens was in his room on the third floor of Station Gloucester when he heard the helicopter land. He looked out his window and saw Paradis, Brad Willey, and a couple of other men walk to the helicopter and unload the bodies. Stevens says that scene was absolutely devastating to watch.

~

Paradis then called the Quirk family. Maureen answered the phone, and Paradis broke the bitter news as best he could, telling her that her dad's body had been found washed up in Nahant. Maureen, who had held out hope despite the long odds, was stunned. Her brother Brian and mother, Audrey, were at home with her, but rather than tell them immediately, she knew she'd need help. She ran next door to Don Lavato's wife, Marilyn, and told her what had happened, saying she needed her at the house. "Marilyn was close to Mom, and I wanted her there when we broke the news. It was awful. Both Brian and Mom were inconsolable."

The devastating news was just as bad for Frank III, who was halfway across the world, stationed as a marine in Okinawa. "I was marching my troops when the captain called me in," says Frank. "At the time I was a lance corporal, and I was up for a promotion to corporal, so I thought that's why he wanted to see me. When I saw the chaplain in his office, I knew this wasn't a promotion. They told me, 'Your father had an accident, and his body was found. There was also an unidentified body found, and there are still people missing.' I ran out of the office and found a phone. It was hard to get through because so many lines were down in New England, but after a couple hours, I reached Maureen. The first thing I said was, 'Is Brian alive?' Brian and Dad were inseparable, and he was always on the boat with Dad. I had no idea how bad the storm was, and I thought Brian might have been aboard.

"The guys in my platoon got all my stuff packed up for me, and I flew from Okinawa to mainland Japan. Then I flew to San Francisco but had trouble getting to the East Coast because airports were a mess from the snow. Finally I got to New York. There were no flights to Boston, so I tried the trains, but they were all filled. Eventually the Red Cross helped me and got me a pass for a train. I was exhausted mentally and physically but still could not believe a storm sank the *Can Do*."

After three days of travel and delay, young Frank arrived in Boston and was absolutely shocked by all the snow. "There was snow everywhere, huge mounds like I've never seen before. Boston looked like a war had been fought there, with National Guard trucks trying to clear clogged streets. Don Lavato used his police identification to drive, and he came down to Boston and picked me up and brought me to Peabody. The whole thing was surreal."

~

Shortly after the helicopter brought Frank's body to Station Gloucester, it was driven to a local funeral home. Frank's brother went there to make the final identification. Frank's face had a huge gash in it, and part of an ear was sliced off. These injuries were probably caused when the windshield broke rather than from his being washed onshore, because Wilkinson's head had no major cuts. While Frank had downplayed his injuries on the radio to Mel Cole, they were in fact serious, and that explains why he mentioned he was getting tired from loss of blood.

On Wednesday afternoon, about the time the bodies of Frank Quirk and Don Wilkinson were being driven to the funeral home, more grim discoveries were made. The bodies of Kenny Fuller and Dave Curley were found washed up in Marblehead, on Devereux Beach and Goldthwaite Beach, respectively. Tattered pieces of the *Can Do*'s life raft and a box of flares were also found. Only Charlie Bucko and the *Can Do* itself were still missing.

~

We can only speculate about the last minutes of the four men's lives. One thing for certain, however, is that after they spent a night eluding death, the sea got the upper hand, like a predator relentlessly pursuing its prey. During the height of the storm, waves assaulted and yanked the boat, ceaselessly trying to part the *Can Do* from its anchor. The predatory sea had stalked the boat, trapped it, and in those last minutes finished the job before the light of day could offer any hope of help.

More than likely, the line holding the anchor slowly weakened where it rubbed against rocks. When it broke, the *Can Do* was doomed. The boat might have capsized immediately, or it might have been swept along with the seas before eventually crashing into a ledge or being toppled by the thundering waves.

The fact that four bodies were found outside the boat indicates they may have had a few seconds of precious time to scramble out on the deck and jump ship. Mel Cole's last conversation with the men mentioned how some of them were down below in sleeping bags trying to ward off hypothermia. If the boat had capsized in an instant, they likely would have been trapped, and their bodies would still have been in the hull of the *Can Do*.

There were still so many unanswered questions. Did the men have time for a last farewell? Did they get the life raft inflated? Did they try to stay together in the water? Did they ever discuss using Frank's gun if the anchor line broke and they knew death would follow? And most important, where were Charlie Bucko and the *Can Do*?

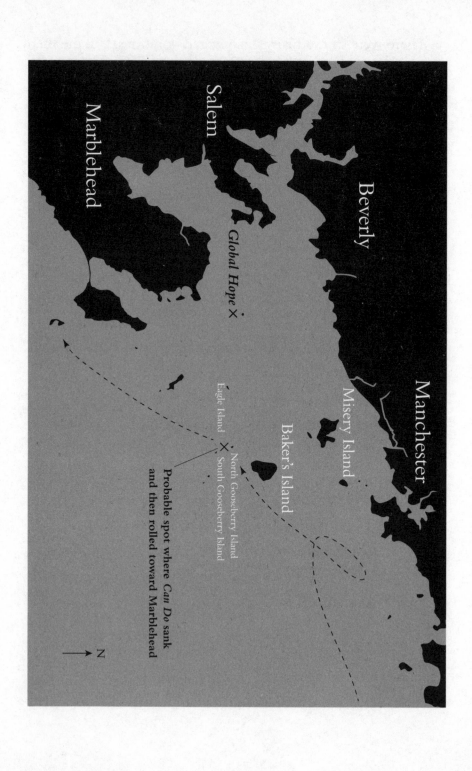

THE WEEK AFTER

While the families of Wilkinson, Fuller, Curley, and Quirk were grieving and in shock, Charlie Bucko's fiancée, Sharon, alternated between the depths of despair and glimmers of hope. Logic told her the love of her life was gone, but because Charlie had not been found, she could not—would not—close the door on a miracle. Maybe, she thought, he had somehow made it to a secluded section of shoreline, injured but still alive. Or maybe the *Can Do* was now high and dry on some secluded, overlooked rocks and Charlie was alive but trapped inside.

During Monday night and early Tuesday morning, she listened to the radio scanner, sick with worry. The reception was poor, and she could only pick up bits and pieces of what was going on, but at least she knew Charlie was alive. Then when communications ceased, she went through the same agonizing wait as the other family members, praying that the men would be found. She somehow got through Tuesday, cursing the snow and wind that still blasted down on her Gloucester apartment.

Tuesday night she was back listening to the scanner, this time trying to follow the progress of the helicopter pilot as he searched the dark seas for any sign of the *Can Do*. And on Wednesday morning, she sank even lower, learning that the bodies of the other crew members had been found.

Sharon had not slept in over forty-eight hours. She was just nineteen years old, and the thought of Charlie being dead was more than she could bear. Just two days earlier, she and Charlie had been planning their May wedding, and now she was terrified that all was lost. She remembers that Wednesday morning like it happened an hour ago. At dawn she called Gloucester Station, and Mike Paradis said, "It doesn't look good." He asked Sharon to call back a little later.

When she called the second time, Paradis said, "I'll be right over."

He arrived at Sharon's door just twenty minutes later, pale and wrung out from exhaustion. Paradis took two steps into Sharon's apartment, stopped, looked her in the eye, and said, "They ran into trouble. Frank's and Don Wilkinson's bodies have been found. We don't know what happened, but resign yourself that Charlie is not coming back. There's just no hope for him."

Sharon screamed, "Get the boats out there and find him!"

Then she pounded on Paradis's chest and shouted, "I know Charlie's alive—he's probably washed up on some island, just waiting to be rescued. You've got to find him!"

Explaining that he was doing everything in his power to find Charlie, Paradis told Sharon he would keep her updated. After an awkward silence, the station commander left, not wishing to lie and give Sharon false hope.

Sharon sat alone in the apartment, shaking from the emotional pain that left her feeling ice-cold. For comfort she had Charlie's dog, Radar, a German shepherd he had bought because it was abused. Sharon thought about the name Radar and the irony that it was the radar failing in the storm that first caused problems on the *Can Do*.

Sharon knew she needed someone to lean on, and although she and her father were not particularly close, she called him and said, "I need you." He came right over, and they waited together in what Sharon describes as the most awful hours of her young life.

~

It wasn't any better for Charlie's parents, who lived in New London, Connecticut. "We found out something was wrong," says Eleanor Bucko, "when we called Charlie's apartment on Tuesday to see how he was making out during the storm. We had no idea he'd be out at sea, because he had left the Coast Guard. Sharon told us he went out on the *Can Do* and that the boat was missing. I was stunned. We wanted to drive to Gloucester immediately, but because of all the snow, it was impossible. Then on Wednesday, we learned they found the other bodies, and we just decided to wait."

Eleanor held out hope, as did Charlie's younger sister, Joan. "When they told us he was missing, it was just incomprehensible," recalls Joan. "I thought that since he made it through Vietnam and had even been shot twice, he could somehow make it through this." Charlie's father, Frank, however, felt differently. He had seen the power of the sea while serving in the navy and knew that only a miracle could have kept Charlie alive through the storm. And so the family prayed for a miracle.

~

Barry Chambers and his Atlantic Strike Team had endured a cold Tuesday night aboard the *Global Hope* and welcomed the sunshine on Wednesday morning. They had many long hours of work ahead of them, but at least they wouldn't be battling the snow and winds.

Chambers still wasn't sure exactly how much oil was on board the tanker, but early estimates were approximately 80,000 to 150,000 gallons. He knew there was a potential for a significant oil spill, particularly if weather conditions deteriorated, causing new cracks in the tanker's hull. He ordered larger capacity pumps and open water barrier booms. When the booms arrived, Chambers had them placed around the stern of the vessel to contain escaping oil.

On Friday, divers confirmed there was a four-foot gash at the rudderpost, but they also saw that the hull had multiple cracks throughout its length. In addition, the rear end of the keel had been ripped off the hull, rupturing some of the fuel tanks.

During those first three days, Chambers and his men worked almost nonstop, with very little sleep. He found that the *Global Hope* was not well maintained, and his written report said "she appeared to have been worked hard, with a bare minimum spent on upkeep." The description sounded like that of a mistreated old horse, still moving but neglected.

The ship's captain was still on board the tanker, but since he was no longer needed, he left the vessel on Friday and got a hotel room in Salem, where he wisely kept a low profile.

~

Over the coming days, the estimate of oil on board the tanker jumped to 270,000 gallons and later was revised upward again to 340,000 gallons. Barry Chambers and the Atlantic Strike Team had been successful pumping out approximately half the oil on the tanker into a barge, but some of the heavier-grade fuel could not be moved because it had to be heated first. By Sunday, February 12, the Coast Guard estimated that 10,000 gallons of heavy oil had washed ashore and another 30,000 had washed out to sea. Oil-fouled birds were dying in the vicinity of Salem, and the thick black goo had settled on the north-facing coastline of Marblehead. Some homes' roofs and windows were covered with oil, carried there by the blizzard's wind. Even as far away as Wellfleet, on Cape Cod, oil globules washed ashore.

On Monday, February 13, efforts to free the tanker by salvage companies proved futile. The tugs wrenched the tanker around to a new position, but its stern was still firmly in place on the rocks.

Barry Chambers had a rough week on board the tanker. His body's resistance had been weakened by the long hours toiling on the cold metal ship, and he came down with a nasty case of the flu that he couldn't shake. Chambers and his men had done all they could to stop the flow of oil, and it was about time to pack up and turn the operation over to a private salvage company. Before he left, however, he met Gard Estes at the Cape Ann Marina, and the two men discussed the *Can Do*. The pilot boat and Charlie Bucko had still not been found, and the Coast Guard had called off the search.

Estes and Chambers talked about potential locations where the *Can Do* might have sunk. Chambers had a pretty good track record of finding lost vessels: after the 1975 sinking of the SS *Edmund Fitzgerald* on Lake Superior, Chambers helped pinpoint the wreck. (The last words from the captain of the *Edmund Fitzgerald* had a familiar ring—he had lost his radar, and he radioed that "these are one of the worst seas I've ever been in" and "we are holding our own.")

Now Chambers worked with Gard using charts, wind speeds, and sea conditions in conjunction with listening to Frank's words on the audiotape, trying to determine the *Can Do's* location. Chambers soon came to the conclusion that the vessel might be found south of Baker's Island, close to shore near Marblehead Neck.

The Coast Guard had searched south of Baker's Island, but perhaps they missed a clue. Frank's friends would give it another look, just as Frank had done when he went back out to the *Chester Poling* for one last attempt to recover the body of the drowned seaman.

WRECKED BOAT,
WRECKED LIVES

On Monday, February 13, funeral services were being conducted for Frank, Kenny, Don, and Dave. But Sharon and the Bucko family were left in a hellish limbo, now resigning themselves to the widespread belief that Charlie was dead. Most everyone who knew Charlie was aware of his mantra that the best chance of survival meant sticking with the boat, and they felt certain his body was trapped inside the *Can Do*. But with no signs of the boat, there would be no body. On that sad Monday, Charlie's parents could not bear waiting in New London any longer. Mrs. Bucko had a feeling Charlie would be found within the next day or two. "The whole prior week had been a nightmare, as if we were in a slow motion, tragic movie, and now I knew Charlie was going to be found. I told my husband, 'They're going to find Charlie, and we should drive up to Gloucester.' I think it was a mother's intuition."

When they arrived in Gloucester, they spent some time with Sharon and packed up a few of Charlie's belongings. Then they went to the Coast Guard station, but there was no news. Next, they stopped in a pub to get a drink, and while they were there, a group came in who had just been to a service for one of the other men. The Buckos told them who they were, but nobody knew what to say. The group just stopped talking, and the Buckos could tell how uncomfortable the group was, so they left and returned to their hotel.

On Wednesday, February 15, friends of Frank's launched an aerial search to try to find the missing boat. Retired Delta Airlines pilot Robert Ward rented a small plane at the Beverly Airport. He and Coast Guard coxswain John Burlingham began making slow runs up and down the coast, concentrating on an area southwest of Baker's Island, the region suggested by Barry Chambers. Looking down into the seas, they thought they spotted the black hull of the *Can Do* in about twenty feet of water between Marblehead Neck and Tinkers Island. The location was approximately three nautical miles southwest of Baker's Island.

Ward and Burlingham made several passes in the plane and became convinced what they saw was in fact the *Can Do*, sitting upright on the ocean floor leaning to its port side.

On Thursday four members of the Essex County Sheriff's Department Search and Diving Team donned their gear and boarded the Beverly harbormaster's small boat for the run down to Tinkers Island. The team consisted of dive master Richard Peverada and divers Steve Archer, John Riley, and Norman "Dugie" Russell. Russell had worked with Frank on several search and rescues, so this was a difficult dive for him to make. "It was the first time I was diving to a vessel where I knew the boat and the captain," says Russell.

Large swells were rolling in from a distant storm, and it was a bitter cold day. When they arrived at the location of the *Can Do,* they could not see it from their boat because of poor visibility in the water. Russell, Archer, and Riley went down first to find the exact location and make sure it was the *Can Do.* Visibility was about three or four feet. They found the boat in about twenty-five feet of water. Russell swam to the stern and saw the ghostly outline of the words *Can Do,* and "immediately got a chill up my spine, and it wasn't from the cold water."

The superstructure and most of the deck had been ripped from the boat, and there were jagged pieces of metal protruding everywhere. The bow was buckled in, twisted toward the port side and pushed back for a full seven or eight feet like a pleated skirt. Russell thought it looked as if the boat had surfed down a giant wave right into a rock: "The stainless-steel railing around the boat was banged to hell, and everything that wasn't bolted down had been torn away. There were dents all along the hull. It appeared as if the boat had been tumbling over and over on the rocks. Nothing remained of the beautiful mahogany furnished quarters below."

The divers then groped along the topside of the hull and came to the dark opening of the engine room. As the sea tossed them from side to side, they held on to the hull as best they could to prevent themselves from being impaled on the jagged metal. Upon entering the engine room, John Riley reached for something to hold on to, and he realized he had grabbed Charlie's foot. Charlie was floating lifeless in the water, dressed in a black wet suit and a jacket, with his arms outstretched.

The men tried to extract Charlie from the engine room, but a ladder and cables prevented them from doing so. To Russell it seemed as if the predatory sea did not want to relinquish Charlie and would make life miserable for anyone who tried.

Russell and his crew did not have any tools to cut the cables, so they got back on their boat and returned to Beverly and secured bolt cutters and a hacksaw. When they returned to the *Can Do*, Archer and Russell went down again. Russell started cutting the ladder with a hacksaw while Archer used bolt cutters on the cables. Because of the swells, Russell was cutting with one hand and holding on to the ladder with the other. At one point he felt a stabbing pain in his neck, and although he didn't know it, he had just slipped a disc. The men finally got Charlie's body up on the boat and motored back to Beverly.

~

Finding the wreck confirmed the suspicion that the *Can Do*'s anchor line broke, leaving the vessel at the mercy of the roaring waves. Charlie was down in the engine room, trying to restart the pilot boat's power, when the anchor line gave way. Now, instead of having its bow into the seas, the *Can Do* was likely spun around 180 degrees by the wave that broke the anchor line. The next wave, or one soon thereafter, drove the boat, bow down, at a speed of twenty to thirty miles per hour, into solid rock.

Once it slammed into the granite bottom, the boat would have pitchpoled, with its stern lifting over the bow and crashing down, leaving the *Can Do* capsized. By this time the men, except Charlie, had either jumped overboard or been swept out of the pilothouse. Charlie, mercifully, may have been killed instantly by the force of the impact, when his head slammed into the engine or the hull. If he somehow avoided this fate, his consciousness would have lasted no more than a couple of minutes. He'd suddenly have been upside down, and the seas would have poured in through the engine room's only exit.

In shoal water, the boat would have continued rolling, being pushed violently by each breaking wave, and Charlie would have become totally disoriented. Charlie literally would have been tumbling with the boat, unable to fight his way out of the cramped and flooded engine room. Whatever air he was holding in his lungs would have been replaced with seawater when he could no longer hold his breath, and his fight would have been over.

Although the boat was found by Tinkers Island, that may not have been where it first capsized. There was enough buoyancy in the vessel and the waves were so powerful that it easily could have been pushed in the direction the waves were going, which was to the southwest. If that was the case, the boat would have originally capsized somewhere to the northeast where there was shoal water. Drawing a line on a nautical chart from where the boat was found back up to the northeast toward Baker's Island, it's logical to conclude that the *Can Do* was at anchor at the ledges and islands known as the Gooseberries.

~

Mr. and Mrs. Bucko were still in Gloucester when they heard reports that Bob Ward had spotted the overturned *Can Do* from the air. Eleanor knew her intuition was right and that Charlie would be found inside the boat, but the wait in Gloucester had become unbearable. She and her husband decided to head home and let the local funeral parlor arrange for the body to be sent to New London. When Eleanor arrived at home, the phone rang and it was Mike Paradis, saying, "Why did you leave? You've got to come back and identify the body." Eleanor told him there was no way they were going back.

The Buckos made a wise decision—the last thing they needed was to view Charlie's body after it had been in the ocean for a week and a half. It was tough enough for them when the funeral director called. "When the funeral home had Charlie's body," says Eleanor, "they called me. The man asked if we would mind if they removed the lining from the casket—he said Charlie's body had swollen up too big to fit inside."

Sharon also learned Charlie's body had been found from Mike Paradis. "He did the tough thing," says Sharon, "and came to me in person. He simply said, 'They found Charlie's body.' I just started beating on his chest and screaming. It was just too much. I look back now, and I think about Mr. Paradis. That poor man, he was so good to us. He was suffering just like I was."

FAREWELL

After Charlie was laid to rest, Sharon fell into the trap of drinking to dull her pain. Sharon's battle with grief and alcohol was just as courageous as Charlie's fight for survival on the *Can Do*. That summer she knew she needed to stop, and she began taking steps. First she stopped drinking alone and then she started staying away from certain people who seemed to trigger more drinking. Then she quit altogether when she realized the alcohol wouldn't really dull the pain, intuitively understanding that only time would. She learned that the grief might ease, but the feeling of loss would never go.

There was one night, not long after Charlie died, that Sharon thought he tried to comfort and reassure her. "I remember one evening I woke up out of a sound sleep with him calling me. He was sitting on the edge of the bed next to me. He told me it would get better, that he was okay, and that I'd see him again. Then he was gone. He had said what he had to say, and he just disappeared. I never even got to touch him."

Sharon says the other strange thing she experienced was when she tried to reread Charlie's manuscript, *The Boat Job*. "It was as if he was writing about what happened the night he died on the *Can Do*. There were just so many parallels: a winter storm, the windshield on a boat being blown out, and a body found later in the capsized boat. How did he know these things? He never told me he had a premonition, but something was certainly going on."

Gard Estes also had an unnerving experience. "A couple months after the men died, I was in my apartment all alone when I looked up, and there they were: Frank, Charlie, Dave, Don, and Kenny. Frank walked up to me and put his hand on my shoulder and said, 'Gardy, I've got to tell you something.' Just then, somebody knocked on the apartment door, and the men vanished. This was not a dream. I was wide awake. Other people have had something similar happen, but they asked me not to give their names."

Just as Sharon continued to wear the engagement ring Charlie gave her, Gard Estes, Louis Linquata, and Warren Andrews found ways to make sure no one forgot about Frank. Gard and Louis did so anonymously, placing a wreath of flowers at the Fisherman's Memorial every February 6 with a note that read *To the men on board the* Can Do.

Warren Andrews took a different approach in remembering

Frank. Warren didn't want the last audiotape about Frank to be his friend's last words from the final transmissions from the *Can Do*, and instead created a tape about Frank's life. He presented Audrey with the tape, and she labeled it with the words *My husband, Frank Quirk*.

On the tape, Warren's voice is rich and deep, full of warmth and good humor. It's clear he loved Frank like a brother. The tape must have taken days to make, because Warren put his heart and soul into it, first organizing his thoughts before recording, then adding touches of background organ music, similar to that used by a church choir.

A first-time listener might call some of Warren's phrases old-fashioned, but he was just being Warren, and his message was sincere. He began his recording by saying, "A fellow recently asked me how well I knew Captain Frank Quirk of the pilot boat *Can Do*. I asked him if he had about twenty-four hours. Seeing he didn't, I said, 'Okay, pull up a chair, and I'll try to cap it all up in about twenty-five minutes.'" Warren then warms to the task, sounding like a retired sea captain rather than a blind shipping control radioman. He describes the many happy days he spent with Frank on board the *Can Do*, as well as Frank's visits to Warren's communications room, about which Warren comments, "People would kid Frank when he'd come up to see me and say, 'Going to see your chaplain, hey?'"

Most of the recording is about various rescues Frank was involved in and how he'd go out of his way to help fishermen and boaters who needed a hand. Warren chuckles, recalling the many calls he made to Audrey, telling her, "Frank will be late coming home tonight"—the same message given before the *Can Do*'s final voyage.

The best part of the tape is Warren relating one of the high points of his life: the time he got to drive the Coast Guard forty-one-footer. "When the Coast Guard got the new four-one-three-five-three, Frank knew how anxious I was to get aboard the new craft and check it out. The CO, Frank, and I got aboard with the coxswain. Once we cleared the mouth of Gloucester Harbor, the coxswain slid out of the seat, and Frank said, 'Okay, Mr. Andrews, you claimed you know Coast Guard boats; get up here and show us.' Well, I climbed into that seat with Frank on my left and the CO on my right giving me steerage instructions. I grabbed that wheel and those throttles and had the time of my life for the next forty-five minutes. That was Frank, always doing something for somebody else."

Warren later commented that God must have needed a good captain, so he took the very best. Then, in a soft voice, Warren said a final farewell to his friend. "Well, God bless you, buddy, and keep a strain on that towline."

EPILOGUE

Looking back at the dramatic rescue attempt performed by the *Can Do*, one can't help but consider how the captain of the *Global Hope* set everything in motion. When the blizzard first started, the *Global Hope* captain was warned that he was "dragging anchor," or drifting. The captain responded that, no, he was still in the same position. That was not true, and the *Global Hope* drifted into a ledge, putting a crack in the hull. Then the captain panicked and called the Coast Guard, shouting, "Our hull is broken! We are in a dangerous position!"

Even after the ship's hull was cracked, the crew on the *Global Hope* were never in any real danger. The ship was in only about twenty feet of water, resting on the bottom, in no jeopardy of sinking. Barry Chambers, the first non-crewmember to board the *Global Hope* after the storm subsided told this author, "That captain cried wolf." Barry is right: if the captain hadn't panicked, the forty-four-foot motor lifeboat would not have left Gloucester and gotten lost in the storm, which in turn caused the *Can Do* to try to help. The entire incident is a good lesson in how one bad decision—by the captain of the *Global Hope*—can have devastating consequences.

The following entries are thoughts from those associated with this tragedy, as well as a short summary of what happened to Brian Quirk:

WARREN ANDREWS

Warren passed away in the early 1990s. In an interview a few years after the blizzard, he said, "If only we knew what was happening to the *Global Hope*, all this could have been averted. But the fact is we didn't know, and there were thirty-two men on board whose lives could have been in danger."

Warren's son Ken related the following about his dad: "The Coast Guard had so much respect for my father, and they knew how close he and Frank were, so they gave him the life vest Frank was clutching when he was found. That life vest was like the Holy Grail to my father; it meant the world to him."

BILL CAVANAUGH

Bill is currently in the Coast Guard Auxiliary and is the director of technology for the Chester Academy in New Hampshire. "Going out to the *Chester Poling* in those seas made me consider my obituary, and I remember at eighteen there wasn't much they could put in it. Prior to the *Chester Poling* and Blizzard of '78, I used to think nothing could happen to me—those experiences sure made me think otherwise."

GARD ESTES

Gard passed away in 2017. Here are some of his thoughts on the tragedy: "Frank did so many things for all of us. It's impossible to describe him except to say he was special. It was very difficult losing those five men; I was good friends with them. For years I've had a wooden sign Frank made, which had a carving of the *Can Do* and a tanker on it. I kept it up in my attic, because I couldn't handle looking at it every day. But on the twenty-fifth anniversary of the blizzard, I hung the sign in my garage, where I can see it every day. Now I look at it and smile. I can still see the black hull of the *Can Do* coming up the Annisquam River and Frank at the wheel."

Gard and Louis Linquata never forgot the men who searched for the *Can Do* and those on the boat. In fact, this writer first became aware of Gard's friendship with Frank when he came across a notice in the *Gloucester Times* on the twenty-fifth anniversary of the blizzard. It read:

> *In Memory of the Pilot Boat* Can Do *and its crew, Captain Frank Quirk, Donald Wilkinson, Charles Bucko, Kenneth Fuller, David Curley.*

> *Special thanks go out to the U.S. Coast Guard and all personnel of the 41353, 44317, 95 Cutter* Cape George,

210 Cutter Decisive, *Helicopter Pilots, Strike Force Team.*
Your efforts will always be remembered.

"We Gave It Our Best Shot"
Gard Estes, Louie Linquata

RICH FITCHER

Rich Fitcher has retired from the Coast Guard and now lives and works on Cape Cod. "The blizzard changed my outlook on life due to the near-death danger we experienced. I cherish every day as not many others do. To this day I can recall the fifty-five-plus-degree rolls we took on the *Decisive*. Our faith in the CO and bridge crew was unquestioned as we engineers kept things going down below. Teamwork got us through the storm, and the men on that ship had an unmatched camaraderie that can't be fully explained in words."

DENNIS HOFFER

Dennis Hoffer served in the Coast Guard for twenty-one years and then became a corrections officer in Massachusetts. "Even before the blizzard, I admired Frank. I can remember being on the *Cape George* one winter when we were tied up in Gloucester. The inner harbor was all iced in, and Frank came by in the *Can Do* and broke all the ice behind the cutter so we could back up without any problem. A few years later, when I bought my first boat, I named it the *Can Do*. That's how much I thought of those guys."

Bob McIlvride

Bob is currently a software technical writer living in Canada. Soon after the blizzard, he transferred to a Coast Guard ice cutter, seeing duty from Alaska to Antarctica. He decided to leave the Coast Guard after four years of service. "The Coast Guard was beginning to do more law enforcement and less search and rescue, and I was uncomfortable with the new rules. I got my fill of adventure on the high seas, and there were other things I wanted to see and do in life." He then traveled the globe, working in such distant countries as Thailand and Chile, while continuing to advance his training and knowledge of Transcendental Meditation and earning his master's degree in technical writing.

"The experience of the blizzard sobered me, but it also helped reinforce my belief that if you have faith in yourself and God, you can move ahead even when the way is not always clear. Losing Frank Quirk was a huge loss to the Gloucester community—he was so well respected."

Brian Quirk

Such a big part of Brian's day-to-day activities was tied to the *Can Do* that when the boat was gone, part of him went with it. He tried to fill the void in some measure by renaming his Boston Whaler the *Can Do* and painting it the same color. Cruising around Gloucester Harbor, Brian became something of a loner, rarely taking friends with him on his outings.

In 1981, after Audrey Quirk sold the salvage rights to the *Can Do*, what was left of the vessel—mostly a twisted hunk of steel—was raised from the bottom of the ocean. "We watched," said Frank III, "along with lots of other people, as the *Can Do* was towed under the Beverly-Salem Bridge and up the North River. Brian was really upset. He kept saying they never should have touched the boat. He talked about sneaking back at night and cutting it loose. I didn't like seeing the boat raised, either, but there was nothing we could do. I tried to tell Brian that the real *Can Do* was gone forever, and that was just a hunk of metal. Maybe I wasn't very convincing."

That last sentence from young Frank showed that although it was painful, he had accepted the loss of his father, simply because it was beyond his control. There was no one person to blame, no one piece of equipment to fault, and nothing to direct his anger at. How do you get revenge on a storm?

Brian, however, could not accept what happened to his father. The tragedy occurred when he was fifteen, and he simply didn't have the life experiences necessary to help him cope. Before the accident, he had a happy, carefree, and exciting life, and then in one terrible night, it was all gone. Seeing the rusted hull of his father's boat in someone else's control was more than he could bear. It was like watching the family home being carted off by a total stranger. He could not understand that the *Can Do* and all it represented was a manifestation of Frank and when Frank died the real *Can Do* went with him. No, for Brian it was like watching a ghost emerge from the water, and it haunted him.

Sadly, a little over a year and a half after the *Can Do* was raised,

Brian took his own life, never reaching out to his brother to tell him how much pain he was in.

RALPH STEVENS

Ralph Stevens served four years in the Coast Guard. Today he works for the Commonwealth of Massachusetts Shellfish Purification Plant at Plum Island. He remembers how the initial plea from the *Global Hope* spurred everyone into action, without enough thought beforehand. "When something like that happens, people operate on adrenaline rather than taking a step back and analyzing the situation. I understand how in some circumstances there is no time to waste, but in the case of a six-hundred-foot tanker, it wasn't going anywhere in that harbor. We should have taken a step back, and before putting the boats out on the rescue the officers should have paused and looked at the big picture, and let common sense dictate action. Besides going out during the blizzard on the Forty-One, I was on the same boat when we rushed to the *Chester Poling*—I'm lucky we made it back from that one. If it wasn't for John Burlingham's skill handling the boat, we would have capsized. Both times the Forty-One should have never been sent out.

"Losing those guys on the *Can Do* was awful. It was heartbreaking then, and it's still heartbreaking now."

SHARON WATTS

Sharon is now happily married and has children. She has never forgotten Charlie Bucko. "Even though I'm married now with three children, I still wear the diamond Charlie gave me. My husband understands. He is a wonderful, strong man. I feel very fortunate to have found someone so special after Charlie.

"While helping with the research for this book, I was going through an old box from my days with Charlie and in it I found a sketch he drew of the design for the house we hoped to build. It was dated February 5, 1978."

FINAL THOUGHTS FROM THE AUTHOR

I think helping others—no matter what the risk—was ingrained in Charlie Bucko and Frank Quirk. They had each assisted in saving lives long before their attempt to do the same during the Blizzard of 1978. Some people have said to me, "Those guys on the *Can Do* were crazy to go out in that storm." I don't agree with that. Hindsight is twenty-twenty. When the *Can Do* left the dock in Gloucester to try to help the Coast Guard, no one knew that the storm was going to explode into one of the worst blizzards ever recorded. Frank and Charlie were probably thinking about the *Chester Poling* rescue. That too was a blizzard so strong the waves tore an oil tanker in half, yet the rescue was successful.

Frank and Charlie were men of the sea, and in the tradition of courageous mariners, they had to at least try to help those in distress on the ocean. But Mother Nature can be ruthless. Even men with the skill of those on the *Can Do* were no match for the Blizzard of 1978. I agree with Ralph Stevens's comment about how a situation must be analyzed carefully before responding to a distress call. The Forty-Four should have not been sent out.

Today's Coast Guard agrees, and they do a risk assessment before committing men and women to venture into the teeth of a terrible storm. They will delay a rescue if they think there is a good chance the rescuers will become victims too.

But 1978 was a different time, and it seemed Frank and Charlie had spent their whole lives preparing for this moment. They had helped so many people over the years, they were hardwired to respond. I often think of Frank's words on the radio when they first went out on the ocean that fateful night: *We'll give it our best shot.* That's what they did. They demonstrated true courage not only by attempting the rescue, but in how they handled themselves as their own situation turned bleaker and bleaker. For me, those men on the *Can Do*—even though they lost their lives—were true heroes. They stepped forward when most people would have stepped back. I spend a lot of time on the ocean and in the woods, and it's comforting to know there are a few brave men and women who will try to help others if we are in serious trouble.

GLOSSARY

AID: a buoy; a floating object anchored to mark a channel or hazard and assist in navigation on the water

BOOT CAMP: initial, intensive training, usually in the military

BREAKWATER: an offshore structure protecting a harbor or beach from waves, usually made of stone or concrete

COXSWAIN: the skipper or the one steering the vessel

CUTTER: as used by the Coast Guard, a vessel sixty-five feet or greater, with accommodations on board

DRAG ANCHOR: when the anchor is set but a vessel still drifts, dragging the anchor along

DRAW: the depth of water needed to operate a vessel without grounding it on the ocean bottom

FATHOMETER: a gauge for measuring the depth of water

FOLLOWING SEAS: waves moving in the same direction as the ship

GREEN SEA: a solid wave of water coming aboard the vessel (as opposed to spray or foam)

GROSS TONS: the cargo-carrying capacity of a ship, or the volume of space in the hull and enclosed deck for cargo and fuel

HEAVY SEAS: very rough water with large waves

KNOT: a nautical term used as a unit of speed; equal to one nautical mile per hour

LORAN: long-range navigation based on signals from two pairs of radios to determine location

LORAN-C: an old navigation system that would determine position by using radio signals transmitted by land-based radio beacons

NAUTICAL MILE: approximately 6,076 feet (a little longer than a normal land mile of 5,280 feet)

PITCHPOLE: when a boat's bow goes down in a big wave and that wave then picks up the stern and pitches it over the bow; to capsize end-over-end

RADAR: a detection system using radio waves that locates objects or surface features

SHOALS: shallow areas

AUTHOR'S NOTE AND ACKNOWLEDGMENTS

One of the most exciting aspects of a book project is at the very beginning, long before you type your first word. I'll never forget the moment when I learned that the *Can Do* was much more than another casualty of the blizzard and maybe, just maybe, there was a book to be written.

I first stumbled onto the story during a difficult period in my life, the summer of 2002. My mother was dying of cancer, and I had flown down to my parents' home in Florida to help my dad, who was caring for both my mother and my sister, who had been seriously injured in an automobile accident twenty-six years earlier. At night, to take my mind off the stressful situation, I often wrote a short bit of text for *The Blizzard of '78*, a book of photography I had contracted to do with On Cape Publications. I had copies of the *Boston Globe* from the week of the blizzard and noted that Tuesday's edition (February 7) mentioned that "a 682-foot tanker was reported aground about one mile off Salem Sound. The Coast Guard in Boston said it lost contact with the tanker, with 34 crewmen aboard." In Wednesday's edition, I came across the first reference to the *Can Do*: "A pilot boat that had run to the foundering tanker's rescue had not been heard from since Monday night, when it lost its navigational equipment in towering waves." Thursday's edition seemed to wrap up the event in a short article that said the crewmen of the pilot boat had died and bodies had been recovered.

Those three editions might have been the end of my interest, but a few months later, before giving a lecture at the public library in Norton, Massachusetts, I was looking through some archival material and came upon a special edition of the *Boston Globe* published shortly after the storm. This issue included a more detailed story, and my pulse quickened when I read some excerpts of Frank Quirk's radio transmissions the night of the blizzard. I was amazed: How often do we get to find out what it was like on a boat where all hands were lost? I read the article three times, riveted to Quirk's every word, wondering if more had been recorded.

There was only one thing to do—try to find his family. To my surprise, there was a Frank Quirk listed in Peabody, Massachusetts; I knew it must be the skipper's son. How would he react, I wondered, to a telephone call from a total stranger? Would he tell me the whole episode was too painful and that he didn't want to relive it?

I called Frank and explained that I was an author and I was intrigued by what little I'd read about the *Can Do* and wondered if anyone had written down more of what his father had said on the radio that night. Frank was gracious and invited me up to Peabody so we could talk more. Then, before he hung up, he shocked me by saying, "You haven't heard anything yet; there's a whole tape of my father on the *Can Do* that night." He closed our conversation by surprising me even further: "I've been waiting twenty-five years for your call. I always thought this story needed to be told in its entirety."

In the five days between the phone call and my scheduled meeting, I thought of nothing else but the *Can Do*. I read everything I could get my hands on about the boat and its captain. When I arrived at Frank's apartment in Peabody, he met me at the door and introduced me to his sister, Maureen. The three of us talked about writing, their father, and the night the *Can Do* went down. I knew there was a book here, as I turned my tape recorder on.

Over the next two weeks, I realized that without Maureen and Frank, there would be no book. Not only did they send me off with a box of information, including the cassette tape of their father's communications on February 6 and 7, but also Frank knew the *Can Do* inside and out from his days working alongside his father. Even better, he was kind enough to patiently answer my many questions and hunt down missing information. I came to rely on him not only for his technical knowledge about the *Can Do*, seamanship, and the waters between Gloucester and Salem but also because, over time, Frank became a source of energy. I got into the habit of calling him every two or three weeks to share information, and after each call I felt rejuvenated, eager to return to my writing and research. As my knowledge of the saga of the *Can Do* grew, I realized Frank was the only other person who knew as much as I did about what happened, and together we were finding and fitting together the pieces of this amazing puzzle. Frank had the same strength of character that his father possessed. Warren Andrews had a saying about Captain Quirk that would have fit young Frank equally well: "He's the guy you want by your side when the going gets tough."

~

I would also like to acknowledge the team at Christy Ottaviano Books. Managing editor Jennifer Healey was a real pro and I appreciate all her efforts, as well as copyeditor Ana Deboo and assistant editor Jessica Anderson. And Christy Ottaviano, whom I've worked with on other books, never ceases to amaze me with her attention to detail and her ability to make the story stronger. It has been a real honor to have her as my publisher and editor.

In addition, I would like to thank the people listed below for their help during my initial research into this story. In no particular order they are: Bill Lee, Mark Gelinas, Gard Estes, Louis Linquata, John Burlingham, Bill Cavanaugh, Jim Loew, Tom Desrosiers, Roger Mathurin, Bob Krom, Bob McIlvride, Sally Lanzikos, Herb Fulton, Ellen Fulton, Vern DePietro, Brian Tully, Myron Verville, Gene Shaw, Bob Donovan, Rich Fitcher, Dennis Hoffer, Jim Quinn, Jim Sawyer, John Halter, Sharon Fish, Eleanor Bucko, Joan Bucko, Janice Bucko, Don Wilkinson Jr., Mel Cole,

Brian Wallace, Barry Chambers, Pete Lafontaine, William Webster, Dean Jones, Ron Conklin, Bowen Spievac, Elmer Borsos, Dan McLean, Jim McDevitt, Richard Pettingell, Brad Willey, Larry Zaker, Marty Risard, Doug Parsons, Peter McDougal, Ken Andrews, Don Lavato, Joe Carro, Ellen Keefe, Robert Thompson, Kristin DiRoma, Keith Nelson, Bob Gesking, Wes Dittes, Dugie Russell, and Ralph Stevens.

ABOUT MICHAEL TOUGIAS

"Tougias spins a marvelous and terrifying yarn."
—*Los Angeles Times*

New York Times–bestselling author Michael Tougias has earned critical acclaim for his nonfiction narratives. His books honor real-life, everyday people who rise to face life-threatening situations, make heroic choices, and survive against the odds. Several of his books have been adapted into the True Rescue series, including *The Finest Hours*, which was a *New York Times* bestseller, a Junior Library Guild selection, a Scholastic selection, an Amazon Best Book of the Month, and a Children's Book Council selection; and *A Storm Too Soon*, which was a Junior Library Guild selection, a Barnes & Noble Top Pick for Kids, and a Scholastic selection. *A Storm Too Soon* was also a National Council of Social Studies Notable Book and a Cybils Award finalist.

You can learn more about the author and his speaking schedule at michaeltougias.com.

MICHAEL TOUGIAS'S BOOKS FOR ADULTS

Rescue of the Bounty: A True Story of Disaster and Survival in Super-storm Sandy, with coauthor Douglas Campbell

Overboard! A True Blue-Water Odyssey of Disaster and Survival

Fatal Forecast: An Incredible True Story of Disaster and Survival at Sea

So Close to Home: A True Story of an American Family's Fight for Survival from a U-Boat Attack During World War II

Above and Beyond: John F. Kennedy and America's Most Dangerous Spy Mission, with coauthor Casey Sherman

There's a Porcupine in My Outhouse: Misadventures of a Mountain Man Wannabe

King Philip's War, with coauthor Eric B. Schultz